Diary of Star-Crossed Lovers

Ray Koeplin and Vi Prestegard

Editing and Layout by Bill Vossler
Copyright © February 2024 by Bill Vossler
Bill Vossler Books

Preface

This is the story of two honest and endearing young people who met April 19, 1938, when Violet Prestegard began working on the Koeplin farms, where Ray lived with his parents. Five days later they declared their undying love and got engaged, then married June 27.

Before meeting Ray, Vi, working in Minneapolis and Albert Lea, wrote a number of times that she "went home" with different guys from dances or dates. Which sounds ominous. But that doesn't mean what it seems to mean today, but rather that the gentleman escorted her home. Also comments that she makes infer the truth.

Then she met Ray Koeplin, and everything changed.

From then on, she only had eyes for Ray, and he for her, until four months after their wedding a disastrous accident killed Vi, and left Ray, suffering from staphylococcus pyemia, a sepsis that causes widespread abcesses (curable today.)

Much spelling in this book is original and uncorrected from the diary unless it was patently unclear, as well as the punctuation.

The diary shows not only the love of the pair, but also Ray's great pain and anguish in what he wrote, when, and how. The book also shows how people lived in rural Minnesota during the late 1930s, how much things cost, and the work people had to do.

Characters mentioned in this diary include members of the Anton Koeplin family. As shown, from the left on the front row, Anton (Tony,) or pa; Veronica or Vernie in the diary, married to Art; Mary, married to Malvin Bebilgan, and Mary Koeplin, or ma. Back row is Clara, married to Bubba, Anne, married to Cyril, Eleanor, married to Gordon, Edmund, married to Dot, Ray, Ethel, married to Frank, Liddy, married to Gene, and Katherine, or Kate, married to Fat.

Violet Prestegard began writing her diary on January 1, 1938.

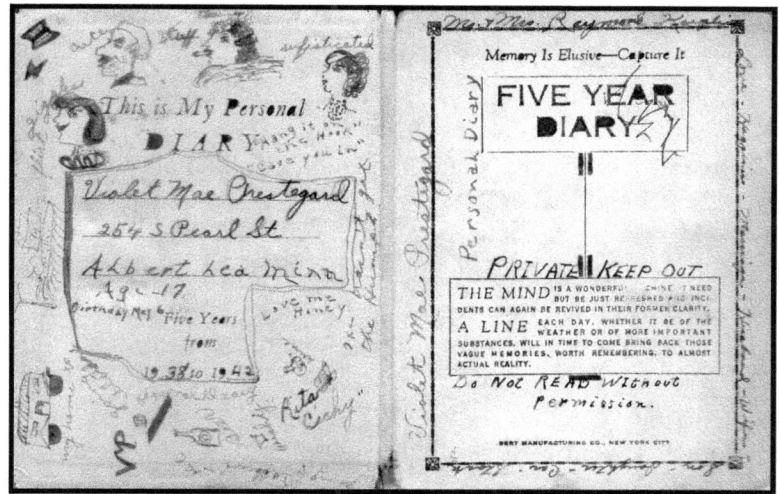

These first pages of Violet's diary show her sense of love for Ray, and later Ray added drawings.

JANUARY 1938 by Vi Prestegard

1. Margie & I went to Red Goldens The Hot Spot to meet some kids and went to Columbia Heights to some dive. Met Frank and went home with him.

2. Stayed home and slept all afternoon. More fun. Some dizzy Jewish boys called me.

3. Went to bed.

4. Rita came back. Was sure glad to see her. Marie, Rita and I went down on Plymouth and then up to Margie's.

5. Frank called and wanted me to go out but I didn't. Connie S. from Fort Snelling also called, but I went to bed. More fun when Rita came over.

6. Rita came over in the afternoon. I had a date with Floyd and we went down town. Had whisky. Rita with Chet. Had one hell of a time.

7. I went over to Rita's and had a chat. Talked about going to Albert Lea to work.

8. Margie, Rita & I went slumming. Down south in Bubbins & Phil's Tavern. Ate in seven different places on Hennepin Ave and almost froze to death. Saw Bob Hanson & Bubba Nye.

9. Rita & I went to show then went over to Rita's. Irene came up.

10. Rita came over we talked & laughed as usual.

11. I was over to Rita's. We ate peanuts & apples. More fun.

12. Margie, Rita & I went to RB. Not much fun. Rita & I went home with Kenny & Johnny. They play at the Camala Club.

13. Rita, Irene & I went down town with Floyd & Otto in the evening to the Jail House & Orchid Café. We got tite.

14. Had a hard day of work. Called Rita and went to bed at 8:30 o'clock. Ate supper at Forum Cafeteria.

15. Went to S. F. With Margie. Met Howie Legacy & went home with him of course. Swell kid not so bashful as I thought. Margie went home with Gordy. Had lot of fun.

16. Rita & I went to a show, very good show. Ate at Malleoff's. Went up to Rita's and ate candy. Irene came up.

17. Rita & I went over to Margie's. We talked and read a very interesting book on sexology.

18. Margie, Rita & I went to show. Not a bad show. Margie met Dorothy and went with her. Rita & I went alone.

19. Floyd called. He is leaving for Chicago Thursday. Stayed home and fixed my coat & went to bed.

20. Rita & I went down on Broadway, got shoes. Went to Daughtry's in the evening and to the Indian Village. Didn't have no fun. Met a Hawaiian boy. He was sure cute.

21. Rita & I went over to Irene's. Made some phone calls. Came home about 10 o'clock.

22. Rita & I walked over to Irene's. Made some phone calls. We walked down to Jack's place on Plymouth. Met Jack a half-breed Negro. And saw Art, ate hot dogs & candy)

23. Rita & I went to the Homewood Theater Saw a good picture Second Honeymoon Came home and went to bed.

24. I went over to Rita. We wrote some cards. Talked, and came home about 10. Al Anderson called about 7:45.

25. Had a date with Al Anderson. we went to Minnesota Theater for a swell picture. Al asked me to marry him. I didn't know I disliked him so well.

26. Rita, Margie, and Irene came up we sat around and talked till about 10:30. Rita got a new job.

27. Rita, Irene and I went downtown and did a little shopping. Went to show. Had supper. And a whisky sour. Came home. State Theater.

28. Mother & Dad wedding Anniversary.

29. Rita, Irene, and I went down to the Calhoun to dance. Boy, what a place, didn't stay over an hour. Then Rita & I went to Daughtry's. Some kids asked us to go home with them but didn't.

30. Rita & I went to Homewood Theater and saw a good picture. Ate a lunch at Malleoff's. Rita came up for a while. She started to work at her new job. Wonder if Al will be here Tuesday.

31. Stayed home went to bed

FEBRUARY 1938

1. Ironed all day but didn't hear a word from Al the louse. Went to bed at 9:30, and Al didn't call.

2. Margie came up we talked and ate apples.

3. Rita & I went shopping. Went up to WDGY and heard them broadcast. Went down to Lucy's. She told me she was going to have another baby. Went to Silver Front to meet Howie & the Bunch. N.E. drank beer and I went home with Howie of course. Met Gordy & Johnny's girl friends. I didn't have such a hot time.

4. Rita came. We talked. Irene called. Howie called at 4:30.

5. Irene, Rita, Marie, Viola, & I staged it up to the SF, and met some kids. We went out to the Stumble Inn. Drank beer. Didn't have much fun. Got home at 3:45.

6. Rita came up and we sat around all day. Rita called Al a blank. Didn't go out.

7. Stayed home & went to bed.

8. Rita & I took a walk. Was over to Irene's a while. Came home about 9:30.

9. Took a walk up to the drug store and mailed a package to Kenny. Was with Marie & Rita.

10. Rita & I went down town and bought a few things. Ate at the Forum Cafeteria. Went to the show, saw Live, Love & Learn. Rita came up.

11. Worked until 10:30. Was so dam tired I could have died. Had a terrible back ache.

12. Rita, Viola, Margie & I went to R.G. then to S.F. I met Chuck Dady. Had a lot of fun Went home with him. Got tight.

13. Went up to S.F. in the Afternoon. I didn't see anybody we knew. Came home about 7:00 Sunday Afternoon.

14. Rita & I went over to Margie's. Sat around & talked. Came home about 9:30.

15. Worked hard all day and went to bed at 8:00.

16. Rita & I went to Lucy's Margurette & Eva was there. Went to the Loring Theater and got home about 11:30.

17. Viola, Rita & I & Margie went to Red Golden's. I met Russ "Mama' s boy". Stayed there until 2:30. Went home with Russ.

18. Viola, Rita, Margie & I went to S.F. Met Howie and the bunch and went to Dayton, Minnesota. Car broke down. Nine of us had to hitchhike. Got home 6:30.

19. Went over to help Rita wash dishes. Drank beer in the basement. Went to the drug store. Came up to my place.

20. Margie, Rita, came over. Talked and went to bed 10:00.

22. Rita, Margie and & I went slumming. Was kicked out of three places. We were in for places on Broadway and five on Hennepin. Saw Floyd in R.G. Got home at 4:30. Was with some kids from the University.

23. Quit my job at Warner's. Left on the 8:30 bus got to Albert Lea at 1:30. Rita & I had a nice trip.

24. Rita & I went up to Herman's Tap room with Mother & Dad. Danced old time. More fun. Jude G. took us home. Saw Donnie Kapple.

25. Rita & I were at Dot's for lunch. Alice was there. Saw Florence. Went to Herman's Tap Room. Went home with Ty Hervey.

26. Went up town with Dot & Rita. Was nothing doing so went out to Lerdahl with my brothers, Harlan and Rita. Met my Love, Donnie Kapple. Went home with him.

27. Went to see about a job but didn't take it. Went up town and walked around. Took pictures. Came home. Went to bed about 9:30

28. Washed clothes. Went riding with Donnie. Had a flat tire. Was down to Dot's. Came home made supper.

MARCH 1938

1. Went out with Donnie. We just rode around. Talked and came home about 9:30. Not him anymore.

2. Went to show with Marlow, Gloria & Rita. Met Al Jenson. Went to Glenville. Got Carroll, who got romantic again. Hope I never see him again. Don't love him.

3. Stayed home alone. Waited for Donnie But he didn't come. Went to bed at 10:00.

4. Went up town with Gloria, Marlow & Harlen, in the Tap Room. Drank beer. Saw Ty. Didn't have no fun.

5. Went with Eddie Iverson. Dot & Hank was in Glenville for a while. Started for Austin at 4 in the morning. Never got home until 11:30 Sunday morning. Slept all day.

6. A beautiful day. Stayed home.

9. Met Eddie up town. Dot was with Stan G. We went to Tap Room, Tenyson's and Stealers. Home 2. Not much fun.

10. Was with Eddie bowling in afternoon. In the evening went to Club Royal Tap Room and Lakies. Stopped in Nick's. Red, Bill, and them was out at Lakies.

11. Eddie & I went to show. Was very tired. Stopped in Steilers. Got home about 10:30.

12. Was up town all afternoon. Dot & I saw Donnie Kapple. Eddie & I & Dot went out in the evening. Had a fight. But it'll be all right.

13. Grandma's 50th Wedding Anniversary. Had a big doings in church. Rita was in. Was down to Dots, Eddie & I. Dot & Smitty went to show. Very good show. Saw Donnie Kapple.

14. Was down to Dots. Finger-waved her hair Went to bed about 8:30 A beautiful day.

15. Dot & I went uptown. Stopped in Tap Room. Went up again in the evening. Didn't have a dam bit of fun.

16. Bubbins came home. Dot & I was up town all afternoon in the Tap Room. Went with Eddie in the evening. Went to Glenville. Dubs was along.

17. A beautiful day. Started work for Armstrong's.

18. Another nice day rained in the evening.

19. Rita & I hitchhiked to Albert Lea. Walked about two miles before we got a ride. Called Eddie and was with him the rest of the evening.

20. Marlowe's birthday. Rita & I took pictures. Had fun and wrote 2 letters.

21. Walked to Rita's. We talked, came home about 9.

22. Stayed home.

23. Stayed home

24. Stayed home. Had company all day.

25. Rita came over we talked. She went home about nine

26. Rita & I walked to Hartland. Eddie looked all over for me, poor guy. We went to New Richland and Manchester.

27. I went over to Rita's we laid around. Tore my coat apart. Took pictures. Rita came over in the evening and helped fit my suit.

28. Stayed home.

29. Stayed home rained all day.

30. Went over to Rita's. Stayed over night because it was raining. Had a hell of a time.

31. Stayed home. Snowed out. Very cold.

APRIL 1938

1. Eddie came out. I was up to Rita's. Went to Hartland then to Albert Lea. I got to feeling good. Rita was with Hans. Didn't have no fun.

2. Had a date with Eddie but I ditched him. Went to Hartland with Johnny A. Rita was with him and I was with Johnny P. in Richland. I drank whiskey, rum & beer all night but didn't get a dam bit tight.

3. Was in Albert Lea and had lunch about 2:30. Got home about 3:30. J. Armstrong came in my room. I kicked him out. Went up to Rita's and we talked. Fell asleep on her bed and never woke up till 8:00. We didn't make supper anyway.

4-5-6. Snowed. Stayed home.

7-8. Rita came over. I was over to Rita.

9. We rode to Hartland with Irvin. Asked some kids to take us to Albert Lea. We went to Avalon & Palm G. Met Donnie K. Got home about 12:30 Sun.

10. Rita came over we talked & ate Peanuts. Sleep a couple of hours. Rita stayed for supper. I packed.

11. Rita came over talked about heaven. I finished packing.

12. Quit our jobs. To Albert Lea. Didn't stay for breakfast.

13. Packed our suitcases. Went to Armstrong with Marlowe & Gloria and some other kids. Had more chances to go places with different kids but turned them down.

14. Took the bus at 7:30. Got to Minneapolis at 12:30. Went up town. Was at Margie's all day. Was up to Mary's at the Silver F. Saw Howie up town. Started for N.F.S. at 12:45.

15. Got to Brandon at 4:30 AM. Nobody up so we sat on our suitcases until someone woke up. I slept all afternoon.

16. Got to Rita's place. Good Friday. Slept all afternoon.

Ray and Vi both have diary entries starting from April 16, the first day Ray saw her in church.

Parts of the diary were written on the particular day and month the diary had printed on it, but Ray used it to write his own diary entries on later days and months, as above, with April 19 on top, and Dec. 12 beneath the line. Vi wrote until the day of the accident.

After Violet Prestegard's death, Raymond Koeplin went back seven months in her diary and wrote what he had thought and felt on particular dates where Vi had already written. He wrote about meeting Vi, their relationship, and experiences that they shared. From here on to October, Vi's comments are in Regular type, *Ray's in in italics beneath.*

17. Went to Alexandria. Got Delores. Got home about 2:00. One hell of a trip. Was still too tired.

Ray's Comments: 17. Saw Vi for the lst time (in church).

18. Went to church with Rita & the family. Went to Rita's grandma's house for dinner. Vern was there. Had a little fun. Met a lot of people.

19. Delores, Rita and I & Paul danced in Millerville but ended up in Brandon and had lots of fun. Met Carl Sheilty not bad. Walter Joos wanted to take me home but Phooey.

Ray's Comments: 19. Met Violet Mae Prestegard Tuesday morning. Delores Cichy introduced her to me. She and Rita came to work for us this evening.

20. Went to Alexandria to take Delores back. I registered for a job. Got home about 6:00.

Ray's Comments: 20. Violet and Rita's first days working here. Mom still sick in bed. She stayed in the kitchen most of that day, I laid mostly on bed.

21. Started to work for Koeplin's. Rita & I both "more fun". Not such a bad place.

22. Worked. Not much to do. Started flirting with the bosses' son & hired man, Rita & I.

Ray's Comments: 22. Started getting acquainted with Vi this evening.

23. Rita & the hired man & I & Ray together this night. Started playing up to Ray, nicest kid I ever met yet.

Ray's Comments: 23. Started flirting with her. The first evening we kept company. Vi waved my hair, & powdered my face. I put hand lotion on her hands. Gave a bottle.

24. Horsed around with Ray. Out with Ray in evening at Bob's joint. Hugged & kissed me. I love him like I never loved anybody ever before. Herbie K. & Ray K. Rita and I played croquet afternoon. Millerville in the evening. Had very much fun.

Ray's Comments: 24. Vi & I played croquet again with Rita & Bernie. First nite I had her out, 1st hugging & kissing we did sitting in a booth at Bob's. First real conversation with her. Vi told me how much she loved me.

25. Washed clothes, more fun.

Ray's Comments: 25. Vi & I sat on the porch. She told me she hated to leave here. She told me she'd stay for a week.

26. Stayed home. Ray & I sat on the porch.

Ray's Comments: 26. Isn't love grand? Vi & I think.

27. Rita went home and I am staying at Koeplin's. Went to dance in Urbank. Herbie took me home. Stayed Overnight.

Ray's Comments: 27. I fell asleep so I couldn't go to the Urbank dance like Vi & I had planned. Violet's first days work here alone. Herb here since last night.

28. Herbie. Ray & I went to Millerville. Drank quit a bit of whiskey & beer. Ate dinner at Ray's sister.

Ray's Comments: 28. Vi & I took Herb home, stayed for dinner at Kates. In the kitchen with her most of the time.

29. Herbie, Ray & I played croquet. Out riding. Ray and I pledged to each other. Hope I am worthy of my "honey."

Ray's Comments: 29. Herb here, the three of us played croquet then went over to Ethel's to get some chick pills for Mom. Vi & I alone at night.

30. Went to Alex with Ray, Herbie, Vernie, Art, Ethel, & Frank. Good show. Stopped in Brandon. It rained all day.

Went to "Inspiration Peak". Took pictures and stopped at Bob's. More fun with Ray. Herbie tried to get fresh with us. How I love Ray. Told Ray how I loved him.

Ray's Comments: 30. Herb here. Took Vi to show in Alexandria with Art, Vern, Ethel & Frank & I. She went home with me. Vi & I up till 2:30 yet when we got home.

MAY 1938

Ray's Comments: 1. Out riding with Art & Vern & Herb had Vi. Told her he'd buy her clothing. She got mad at him at Bob's & then went home with me.

Ray's Comments: 2. Herb went home & was Vi ever glad. Said he was nothing but a trouble maker. Her & I together more & more every day, alone with her every night.

Ray's Comments: 3. Asked her to go to Millerville dance with me. She said, "This time you don't dare to go to sleep though." Cleaned & altered my suit for dance tomorrow.

4. Ray & I engaged. Never thought I could fall as hard in love like I did for my dearest Raymond.

Ray's Comments: 4. Herb came over & we went together. He thought he had her, bought her ticket and she left him sitting. Told me I should go sit in a booth with her. Told me how much she loved me. She and I asked each other to get married, so tonight we proposed. Home with me. Both were feeling good so I said come tell me all this next morning.

Ray's Comments: On May 5, while Mom, Dad and Bernie were milking, Vi came & told me that she meant what she said last night. Her & I started planning. I and Vi up to

Vern, alone with her from noon till 4:30. Told Vern about our love. She thought just like Vi and I did, tell Father Wilkes.

6. My Birthday. Was up to Vernie's all day had whiskey. In the evening Herbie & the bunch came up. Had plenty of beer & so lot of fun. One of the happiest days of my life. Ray and I celebrated my birthday all alone up at Ray's sister's place. More fun. Talked and planned and trid to figure out how we could get married. Told Vern how terribly in "love" Ray and I were. She told us to tell Father Wilkes. Ray and I had already planned that.

Ray's Comments: 6. Went to see Father Wilkes on a sly Saturday. afternoon. He told us we had just as much right as any other couple, & maybe even more to think she would sacrafice her life to take care of me for life.

7. Stayed home. Talked things over with Ray. Planned if we only can marry soon, real soon I mean.

Ray's Comments: 7. Herb here, told him that Vi & I were engaged & were planning to get married. Her & I up in evening till 12:30 planning.

8. Went to show in Alex. Ray, Herbie, Bernie & and Mary's family. Saw "In Old Chicago".

Ray's Comments: 8. Vi & I to show with Mary & Melvin. Mad at us because I was broke & didn't chip in & buy tickets. Vi & I home alone in evening.

9. Ray and I talked tried to figure things out. But it's a hard thing to figure out.

Ray's Comments: 9. Vi & I are together almost every moment she could spare. We'd play croquet & then try to think of a way to see Father Wilkes about marriage.

10. Ray and I went to Millerville. Drank beer & whiskey. Both were feeling plenty good. Nothing doing!

Ray's Comments: 10. Art told the "old man" that I was using dope again & that I was drinking. A dam dirty lie about the dope. Was Vi & I ever mad at Art.

Ray's Comments: 11. Both decided to see Father Wilkes the first chance we'd get, see what he'd say & then we'd tell my & her folks about it. Both praying.

Ray's Comments: 12. Both of us still planning hard. Planning on seeing J.B tomorrow when we'd go to the creamery. She wanted to write her Mom, but told her to wait.

13. Worked. Ray & I went to see Father Wilkes about getting married. He thought it would be all right.

Ray's Comments: 13. Bernie mad at us yet. Got the rest all to go to show for spite. Got the car & money in eve. & then went to J.B. He was in bed and said we'd come tomorrow.

14. Went to church 7:30. Herbie, Ray & I rode around all morning. Drank beer. Told the folks about getting married they almost had a cat fit. And of course the answer was NO. Didn't think I could love a man as much as Ray K. as I do.

Ray's Comments: 14. Vi & I to town to get an owl that Schecks want mounted, then over to J.B. He said we'd have more right to get married than a healthy couple, cause I'd be taken care of always.

15. Left Koeplin's. Hated to leave Ray. Nobody will never know. But only for a while. Here Ray xxxxxxxxxxx kisses.

Ray's Comments: 15. Mom's "ladies aid". Told the folks about us, & did they ever fly off the handle. Nothing doing they said. Herb tried to help us talk them into & Cyril. Too. Cyril told the folks, "Chessus Christ, Ray has just as much rite to get married as you did." That morning the folks told her she couldn't stay any longer here. I'll never forget how we both had to cry upstairs while her and I packed suitcases and then hug and kiss her goodbye. Dad took her to Cichy's.

16. Rita & I hitchhiked to Urbank, Parker's Prairie, Miltona, Alex, and Millerville. Had to walk from Brandon to Millerville. Took 2 1/2 hours. Stayed over night at Gram Joos. Stopped in to see Elnor in Parker's Prairie. How I miss my "love", Raymond Dear".

Ray's Comments: 16. Vi left here. Sat upstairs crying for half an hour. Never felt so blue &in all my life as I did today. Planned harder than ever. Wrote first letter to her.

17. Rita was sick. Slept all day. Went to dance in Urbank, didn't have much fun. Guess because Ray wasn't there.

Ray's Comments: 17. Can't help but bawl every little while. Even Mom & Dad & Bernie miss her. Tried to get $500.00 from the folks.

18. Ray came up after me. Vernie, Art, and Bernie was along. Went to dance in Millerville. Had a lot of fun.

Ray's Comments: 18. Art & Vern took me over to Cichy's and picked up Vi, then went to Millerville dance. Sat in booth at Bob's planning almost all night.

19. Walked up to Vernie's place in the rain. Ray came up and we talked. I stayed over night with Vern.

Ray's Comments: 19. Rained. Both of us met at Vern's place, walked in the rain. Vi stayed overnight there. Her & I together all afternoon, alone. Second dance I took her to, at Millerville. Dad even danced with Vi. Planned hard.

20. In the evening Ray came to Millerville to his folks 40th wedding anniv dance. Lot of fun. Danced with Mr. Koeplin. Ray said he is taking dope again. Made me feel terrible.

Ray's Comments: 20. Art, Vern & I picked up Vi at Cichy's again & went to the folks 40th Wedding Anniversary. Did we ever have fun that night, home at 2:30.

21. Went to Clitherall where Rita started to work. I looked all over hell for a job. But couldn't get anything. Ray came up in afternoon. We took a whole film of pictures.

Ray's Comments: 21. For an excuse I told the folks I had to bring the things she left here, over to Cichy's. Together all P.M. Planned how we could meet tomorrow

22. Went to church. Met Ray after church. He was feeling pretty good. Went to Bernie Buce's place for dinner. They have a very nice home. Martin Craul took us to Urbank. Sat around and drank beer got home about 11:30. More fun.

Ray's Comments: 22. Stayed in town from church, picked up Vi after high Mass then up to Bernie's place for dinner. Martin Craul took us to show at Urbank in evening.

23. Washed a few things out. Mr. Newhouse called and said my job was open. Think of Ray all day.

Ray's Comments: 23. Vi got a job at Alexandria. For 2 weeks, leaving tomorrow. $6 per week. Told me Sunday she'd save so we could get married by a JOP.

24. Wishing I'd see him before going. Started at Elmwood Cottages at Alex. How will Ray find me? Worked all day. Praying Ray come tomorrow. Wished we were married.

Ray's Comments: 24. Today Vi really started her work, cleaning cabins at the Elmwood Cottages eight miles south of Alex, to make enough money so we can get married.

25. Started to clean cabins. Ray came out in the afternoon. He was plastered. Herb & Martin were along too. Got back at 7: o'clock. I was fired. Went to Alex raised Cain. Stayed overnight in Alex at Kehoe's.

Ray's Comments: 25. I don't do a dam thing except think of Vi all the time. Can't see why they had to part us.

26. Got up at noon ate at the Rainbow Cafe. Horsed around town for a bit went to show evening. Delores had to work.

Ray's Comments: 26. Stayed at Bob's from church, there Herb gave me a letter from Vi & he, Martin & I went to see "her". I stayed till 5:30. "She" still loved me as ever. Got fired on account of us three.

27. Went shopping in the morning. Got a ride to Millerville with Fat I. Orsung. Stayed overnight at Ma. Joos. Was to church in evening. Saw Ray but didn't get to talk to him.

Ray's Comments: 27. To Confession & to the Mission. Planning on how I can get to Alex. Sunday to carry out our "Plans". If they don't work nothing ever will.

Ray's Comments: 28. To communion. Set up Vi's picture on the buffet took it down. Second time I did, she took it down & said she burned it up.

29. Was in Bob's. Met Ray and we drank quite a bit of beer. Met Martin Crawl. I was pretty darn drunk. We went to Alex Mart to a show. Ray & I rented a room in the Douglas Hotel. Refused "IT."

Ray's Comments: 29. Met my dearest Vi at Bob's when Butts & I walked to town. Picked up Martin, went to Alex., then up to the Douglas Motel. Stayed overnight.

30. Ray & I got up about noon went to Travelers Inn had Supper. The Sheriff came up about midnight and took Ray & I. I was put in jail until morning They put a vagrancy charge on me.

Ray's Comments: 30. Had in mind to get our marriage license, take the application & get married but it was Decoration Day. Dinner at Rainbow & Supper at Travelers Inn.

31. We had a hearing in the court house. Katie, Ed, Ma & Pa were there and we had to do some quarreling. Ed took us home.

Ray's Comments: 31. This is part of the story. To hell with the rest. Went to Instructions up to June 26. Folks picked us up & we met at the court house. Vi & I had to argue about 3 hours but we won out too. Took us both home.

JUNE 1938

1. Was up to Father Wilkes. Ray and I asked of me Started instructions.

Ray's Comments: 1. We both got up in time for Mass, then went to Father Wilkes. Told us Vi would have to promise to keep her religion & she did.

2. Went every day sometimes twice a Day

Ray's Comments: 2. Morn up to the priest Came home & told us we should both come to Mass & instructions tomorrow.

None of Vi's Entries Are Available June 3-June 26

Ray's Comments: 3. Vi first day of instructions. Vi's Mom letter with $5 to come home. Vi said get married first.

Ray's Comments: 4. Both to instructions again & also Mass. Both think there's something wrong again somebody "against" us again.

Ray's Comments: 5. To church, at dinner, did the dishes, then went out walking cause we thought all sisters came to talk us out of getting married. Elnor, Pa & Art for us.

Ray's Comments: 6. Both to instructions. Over at Mary's, & also over at Ethel's, had lunch there. I'm getting a lump. Only Vi & I know it.

Ray's Comments: 7. Father Wilkes gone for 3 days. Opened my lump--she did with a scissors--today. I looked as disgusted Ma thought I was sorry over it all already.

Ray's Comments: 8. Vi's Mother called from Brandon, Vi & I got her. First tried to talk us out of it but gave in pretty easy when we told her how much in love we were.

Ray's Comments: 9. Vi's Mother left today. Tried to get Vi to go home with her before she went. Vi told her she'd never go. Mom, Vi & I took her to Brand. Left $5.00 for Vi.

Ray's Comments: 10. To Instructions with Vi again. Father Wilkes told us we shouldn't listen to the rest of the family, told us Mom already gave her consent, also Dad.

Ray's Comments: 11. Vi & I to instructions again. Was going to mount an owl, but it was chewed up by mice. Wrote & asked Vi's Mother for her consent to marry.

Ray's Comments: 12. All to church except Dad. Mom stayed in town. Vi drove the car home. Made dinner for Dad then we went out walking, in eve. Out riding.

Ray's Comments: 13. Both instructions at 1:30. Dad building over to Uncle August Roers. Told to come & get him if the rest came home to talk us out of it.

Ray's Comments: 14. Vi & I to Tony Kline's Funeral, first funeral Violet ever was to. Vi & I home alone, folks were to Rosella Rutten's Wedding. Home in the eve. Too.

Ray's Comments: 15. Vi got a letter from her Mother giving her consent to marry & asked Vi what she should send.

Ray's Comments: 16. Instructions Father told us to thank Vi's Mother for giving her consent. Started planning for the Wedding. They want Vi dressed in white.

Ray and Vi got their long-awaited marriage certificate on June 16, 1938, and were deliriously happy.

Ray's Comments: 17. Mom & Vern along with Vi & I to Alex. Got our license & some clothing for both of us. Also the ring. To instructions in P.M.

Ray's Comments: 18. Vi & I to instructions. Father told her to walk in the procession tomorrow. Wrote a letter to Herb. Bought groceries at Fat.

Ray's Comments: 19. All to church except Pa. Vi and I out riding all afternoon, planning—between the lakes. Both talked everything over again eve.

Ray's Comments: 20. Vi & I to instructions. Vi & I planned on having Elreen & Raymond for ushers but J. B. said they weren't old enough.

Ray's Comments: 21. To instructions forenoon & afternoon. Herb came back from cities. Here with Alfred in evening.

Ray's Comments: 22. To instructions in forenoon. Herb came to visit. Herb, Vi & I up till 12 talking. Vi altered suit.

Ray's Comments: 23. Ed & Dot are going to "stand up' for us. Vi & I to instructions, then she helped open a lump, & then we went to Alex. With Ed, Dot & Mom.

Ray's Comments: 24. To instructions again. Bought my Dear Sweet wife-to-be a missal just like mine, so she can watch me & learn soon.

June 25. I was baptized and Mr. and Mrs. Tony Koeplin were my sponsors. Went to confession.

Ray's Comments: 25. Violet Baptized today. Mother & Dad Sponsors. All to confession. Got our marriage instructions.

June 26. I was received into the church. Mr. and Mrs. Tony Koeplin were my sponsor. Didn't got out much before we were married. Between the Sat May 31 to June 26 we were to one dance. There was quite a bit of quarreling and fighting. Ma came up here and stayed overnight. Didn't help much just a little more trouble. And after all we went through we were finally to be married on June 27.

Ray's Comments: 26. Vi made her First Communion at the altar with Mother & Dad. Practiced this eve., got flowers, then over at Ed's. Vi set Dot's hair.

June 27. Ray's only brother Edmund and his wife Dot stood up for us. Ray's niece was flower girl. Ruth Hagedorn Was married at 8 o'clock in the morning. Stopped in at Father Wilkes afterward then went home Had big dinner mostly the brothers & sisters. Father Wilkes Went to Alex for pictures. Group & bust. Dance in the afternoon at the Millerville ballroom. Carroll Julius took in $70 all day.

Ray's Comments: 27. OUR WEDDING DAY! Married my Love, Violet Prestegard, happiest day of my Sad life. Just a small quiet wedding, dance in eve. Music Carl Julius.

PARK REGION ECHO

Date June 30, 38 Page 4
Column 6

PRESTIGARD—KOEPLIN

Marriage vows were exchanged Monday forenoon at St. Mary's church of Millerville between Miss Violet Prestigard and Raymond Koeplin. Father Wilkes read the nuptial mass and performed the ceremony.

The attendants were Mr. and Mrs. Edmund Koeplin. Miss Ruth Hagedorn was flower girl.

The wedding dinner and reception was held at the groom's father's home at which the immediate relatives were present.

Ray and Vi got married on June 27, 1938

June 28. Got up about 9 o'clock Went to a double wedding. Father Wilkes started on his trip. Coming back July 15.

Ray's Comments: 28. Vi & I slept till 9 o'clock then went to a Double wedding. Took in around $70.00 yesterday. Just think one whole day of married life. Isn't it Grand?

How I Love You After Being Married

*I love my Vi,
I think she's Grand:
When I go to a show,
I hold Her Hand.*

*I hold her tight,
Around the waist;
When I get fresh
She slaps my face.
June 28, 1938*

Ray's Comments: 29. Soled Vi's shoes. To Brandon for my samples. Vi & I compared prices with different companies.

Ray's Comments: 30. Vi & I slept till 9:30 again. Wrote to Mcconnon's. Nice congratulations from Vi's Mother.

Ray's brother Ed and wife Dot, who stood up for them, with Ruth Hagedorn, flower girl.

JULY 1938

No Diary entries for Ray from July through August 31. Probably pretty sick. Vi's Entries are more spotty too.

Wed. 20. Ma, Ray & I went over to Ethel's and picked peas. Merrial & Ruthy were along Katie was here in the afternoon. Got our pictures. A package from Grandma.

Thurs. 21. Stayed home and canned beans. Ray & I cleaned them. Lots Of fun. "Dats vot you think," Ma.

Fri. 22. Ray & I went to Alex. Took Merrial & Ruth over to Lydy's. Ray got the job of Mcconnon.

Sat. 23. Tonie was here to fix the lights. Art & Vern here for dinner. Got lights today.

Sun 24. Stayed home all day & slept. Was up at Art & Vern's in the eve. Went to Millerville had beer & ice cream.

Mon. 25. Ruth went home. Canned more peas & beans.

Tues 26. Sewed a little. Ray & Ma went to Parker's Prairie to see Elnor. Was to dance in eve. I didn't have a good time. Came home, Mary & Melvin.

Wed. 27. Rita called. Sewed on Vern dress, Katie & Cyril & Ann & family were here. Art here and fixed the lights.

Thurs. 28. Finished Vern's Dress & Mer.

Fri. 29. Cleaned house. Ray & I were alone. Ma to Vern's.

Sat. 30. Was up to Vern's. Nord, Ray's cousin & his wife were here. Went to Silver Slipper in the eve.

Sun 31. Vern & Art were here. Went riding in the afternoon with Mary & Melvin.

AUGUST 1938

Mon. 1. Ray & I home alone all day. Ma up to Vern's

Tue. 2. Home all day. Helped Ray with his products. Got pretty near settled.

Wed. 3. Home alone all day. Ray & I packed his goods. Vern here in Afternoon. Ma at August's help cooking.

Fri. 5. Thrashed here all day. Vern here and helped.

Thurs. 6. Thrashed in forenoon. It rained in afternoon. Was to confession. Prayers heard, I think Ray or Vi.

Sun 7. Was to communion. Lucille was operated on. Ray, Herb, Ma, & Bubba to Parker's Prairie.

Mon. 8. Thrashed all day. Vern here. Was to Parker's Prairie. To see Lucille. Father Wilkes was there.

Tue. 9. Rained. Herb, Ray & were to Evenville & Elbow Lake and looked at cars.

Wed. 10. Finished thrashing.

Thurs. 11. Ma was up to Vern's all day. Christy was here.

Fri. 12. Ray got his car. Went riding in the eve.

Sat. 13. Ma was over to August. Helped with the cooking.

Sun. 14. Marlowe was up, also Ortin K. Ray, I, Herb, Marlowe & Ortin out riding. Had a case of beer for supper.

Mon. 15. Was to church. Cyril & Ann were here for dinner. In the evening we drove to town.

Tue. Wed. Thur. Fri. Sat. 17, 18, 19, 20. Ray was sick all week. In bed most of the time. Ma Ray & Vern were in Brandon too & got Pills.

Sun 21. All the kids were over to Ethel's for dinner. Ray in bed so couldn't go. He stayed home all week, Ray sick at home all week, Mon. Thru Fri.

Mon. Tue. Wed. Thur Fri. Sat 22, 23, 24, 25, 26, 27. Ray was sick and stayed home all week. Nothing doing.

Sun 28, 29, 30, 31. Making out good. Went to Millerville. Watched the airplane. Was in Bob's.

Ray's Comments: 31. We're planning on moving Ya Ya.

OCTOBER 1938

Nothing in September, and starting here, Ray is writing his feelings about losing Vi, and remembering experiences.

Oct 1 to 17. Weather cold. Retailing & Making out good. We were planning on moving over to Ann & Cyril's other place for $3.00 & we could have brought a cow, pig & 25 chickens. Sent off for furniture Oct 17. There couldn't have been a happier couple than we were. Oh God why did you part us? If it were only God's will to let me die with her.

Oct. 18. Tues. We had in mind to go out selling. Got change from Bob's then got another flat tire. Had one in the AM before we started. Had fixed at Gene's. Got two bits for setting Lidy's hair while I was waiting. She said it was too cold for me to go out & said she wanted to go to Alex to do some shopping while we had money yet, but she changed her mind when she got outside. Then we decided on going over to Ann's & she wanted her to go along with us & look over the house. Ann was herding cows so Vi told me we'd go over to Bob & have our dinner there where it was warm. We got there 11:45. We had three cans of sardines & I had shots & she beers. At 2:45 we left & I drove out of town, then she wanted to drive. At Bob's she told Clara she was going to drive. I made a mistake. We came into Bob's at 12:15 & we left Ann's at the time given above. From out of town she drove as far as the fork straight North from Millerville. There I told her to turn East, go past Cichy's then to Art & Vern's & then home. She answered me in a joke yet. "I'm driving & I'm the Boss today. I'm going to the Shady Haven yet." We kept going West till we got past Paul Klimek's. There she hit loose gravel, & started swaying. I straightened her out the first time, she turned too much the other way again because she thought it swayed too much my way. I hollered to slam on the brakes. She stepped on the gas instead. I pulled the emergency but it was too late & we went down the bank. It was one terrific crash. We went over twice. She grabbed me when she saw we were going over. But she went out of the door on her side & pulled me into her seat. Oh! God Help Me. We were unconscious for 5 or 10 minutes, then I started moving. When I came to & saw the gas dripping & heard the motor running. I kicked till I got the cabinets back so I could turn off the motor. I thought of fire & I hollered at her to crawl away from the car. When I got that shut off she told me "Ray I'm dying". We made an act of contrition & then I kept on trying to get out. My stiff leg was caught & I couldn't get loose. Finally I got out of the car, got her hand from under the car & lifted her out. She couldn't stand. When I asked her if she wanted the priest she said "Yes Ray, a priest and a doctor." I ran up to Paul Klinek's & nobody was home. I called Urbank & told them to send out Father Wilkes, a doctor and help. I even fainted half way up to Klimek's. When I did crawl into their house they weren't home. I looked around, saw a telephone called Urbank & told them to take care of the rest. Mrs. Klimek & her daughter came home. Mrs. Klimek & I ran to where Vi was laying & her daughter drove out to get him. We covered her up & then he came. We picked her up & took her to his house in his car. She laid about three fourths of an hour before the doctor came. I fainted at her bedside. The doctor finally came and looked us both over. I told him to look her over first & he did. When the doctor came to look me over & was through with me, I got up & went over to Vi's bed. Then Father Wilkes came. She confessed & received the last Sacraments. Then the doctor took her to the Parker's Prairie hospital and Fat and I followed. The doctor said she wasn't hurt bad. At 7:30, Pa, Ma, & some of the rest came & the doctor said she wasn't bad then yet. Around 8 they left & 8:15 Mrs. Liebold came, & told me I could go & see her any time I wanted to. I was with her from 6 until 7:30, then they gave us both a hypo & told me I had to give her rest. When I got up to her room & saw her then, I gave up hopes. This was about 8:15. I kept on telling Vi she shouldn't give up, & she told me she wouldn't. She didn't have pain because of the hypo & she talked real nice yet. She told me then to hug & kiss her & I did. She kept on telling me how she loved me & that it was all her fault. I told her not to feel that way about it. Then she started wishing Mother (My Mom) were there so she could tell her that. She asked for Ma three or four times, and then I asked her if I shouldn't notify her folks & if she didn't wish that her Mother were there. Then she told, "Yes, I wish my Ma was here." Outside of that she didn't say anything about her folks. I told her to think of our Lord & the Blessed Virgin & she said she was thinking of them. She said her last prayers after me so nice when I was alone with her. And she kept telling me "Oh Ray! I just hope Baby isn't hurt". She told the nurse that she was pregnant after she heard Dr. Stensrud ask me that. He told me "She's pregnant, isn't she"? I told him "yes". Then he said "about 2 or 3 months" & I told him "yes." Around 10 Ma, Dad & the rest came up. Elnor & Gordon & Della came up earlier. They tried to build up her strength by giving her hypo shots which I suggested, but she was getting weak then already. She always nodded her head when I told her "Don't give up." Around 11, her breath started failing & just before she took her last breath I asked her "You still know me Vi?" & she nodded. Then she closed her eyes with a great big smile on her face. Around 12 she was dead. I stayed with her about 15 minutes yet. She died while I was holding her head & her hands & I kissed & hugged her goodbye just before she died yet.

> **PARK REGION ECHO**
>
> Date Oct. 20, 1938 Pg. 1
>
> ## Bride of a Few Months Killed in Auto Accident
>
> ### Mrs. R. Koeplin Dies From Injuries at Parkers Hospital
>
> VIOLET
>
> MRS. RAYMOND KOEPLIN
>
> **Car Upsets When It Hits Loose Gravel and Young Bride Dies From Injuries**
>
> Mrs. Raymond Koeplin of Millerville, a young bride of only a few months, was fatally injured in an auto accident Tuesday afternoon about 4 o'clock near Inspiration Peak. She died three hours later at the Parkers Prairie hospital aged 18 years.
>
> Mr. and Mrs. Koeplin had made a trip that day to Inspiration Peak and were on their way home when the car struck loose gravel on the road and turned over. Mrs. Koeplin received internal injuries. She was taken at once to the Parkers Prairie hospital for medical aid, but died at about 7:00 o'clock. Mr. Koeplin was not seriously injured.
>
> Violet Prestegaard Koeplin was the daughter of Mr. and Mrs. Theo. Prestegaard of Albert Lea Minn. She came to Millerville last winter and met Raymond Koeplin. A romance resulted and they were married in June.
>
> Funeral services will be held Friday morning from St. Mary's church in Millerville.
>
> Millerville citizens bowed their heads Friday morning to pay tribute to Mrs. Raymond Koeplin who passed away at the Parkers Prairie hospital at 11:00 o'clock Tuesday, Oct. 18. She is survived by her husband, Raymond Koeplin. She was fatally injured in an automobile accident about 4:00 o'clock Tuesday. She and her husband were driving home and struck a ridge of gravel in the center of the road and their car went over the embankment.
>
> Violet Prestegaard was born at Albert Lea May 6, 1920, She was united in marriage on June 27, 1938 to Raymond Koeplin. She was a very popular young lady, loved by all who came in contact with her.
>
> Services were conducted from St. Mary's church Friday morning at 9 o'clock. Rev. Father Wilkes of Millerville sang the Requiem mass. Rev. Theo Kupka of Geneseo, N. D., a friend of the family, was present in the sanctuary. The pall bearers were Ed Roers, John Ritten, Wm. Roers, Herbert Koeplin, Harry Roers, Jr. Aloys Roers and honorary pall bearers were Mrs. Ed Roers, Mrs. Al Roers, Mrs. Harry Roers, Jr., Mrs. Wm. Roers, Justine Roers and Mrs. John Ritten. Cross bearer was Rita Cichy. She is survived by four brothers and her parents.

Vi wanted to learn how to drive, and one day the car she drove hit loose gravel, rolled, and threw her out.
After Vi's death, Ray wrote pages and pages in the diary about the accident and his bereft feelings.

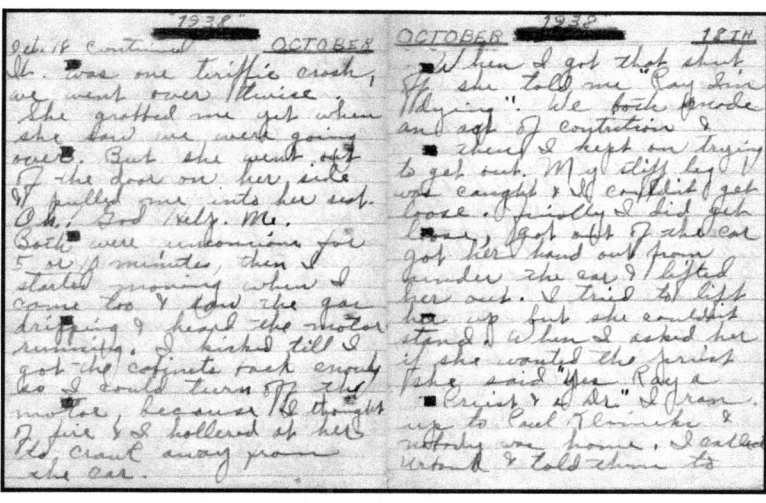

Oct 19. I went home with Fat, Kate, Mom. Dad got 2 pills for me before we left the hospital. Around 7 Vi's folks came. Mr. Mrs. Bubbins & Kenneth. Ma, Dad, Vi's folks, I & Art went to Parker's to pick out a casket. Elnor came down. I suggested the County pay the funeral expenses. In the afternoon Dad, Cyril & I went to Parker's again & he decided to pay it alone after the Board said they'd give only 75.00. Dad & I wanted the one for 150.00 & he was going to pay the difference but they wouldn't allow that. Dad paid it all. Hildgard Lorsung brought pills from Kirland.

"My Dear Beloved Wife"

    Violet May Prestegard
    First a girlfriend of mine;
    Now my Dear Beloved Wife,
    So kind, so true, & fine.

    I met "her" one morning,
    That day I'll never forget;
    The beauty in "her" voice,
    When Good Morning "she" said.

We both fell in love,
With each other right there;
Yes, "she" promised then already,
To help my suffering's bear.

To think how we prayed,
That we could marry real soon;
How the Lord heard our prayers.
We married the 27th of June.

How happy both were,
And enjoyed married life;
I couldn't have been more happy,
Just to think "she" was my "Wife".

How we used to pray & plan
Of all the things we would do;
And to think that almost every plan,
We planned, always came true.

What a pious women she was,
How she used to pray with me,
Now to think "she's" gone & left me,
Yes, gone to Heaven a Saint to be

How I miss her going to bed,
See "Her" kneel right down & pray
Pray for things, then thank Our Lord,
For sending them our way.

For this I thank Our Lord,
For keeping me at "her" side,
To see "her" receive the Sacraments,
And see how nice she died.

So Lord let me suffer,
Then die a happy death like "she";
Let us both soon meet in heaven,
Where we may forever love Thee.

Place me where I can always,
Love my Dear Beloved Wife;
Love Thee above all things;
Then love you both all my life.

I know the Lord is merciful,
And that He still loves me;
That He will soon prepare the way,
For me My Beloved Wife to see

Thurs. 20. A lot of people here. No sleep again.

Fri. Oct 21. Oh God! To think it was my last dry with her. She was buried at nine o'clock at Millerville. I just couldn't get over it. Her folks left around 2 in the afternoon, & Kenneth stayed. My first decent meal at dinner. I didn't sleep more than an hour & during that little time I was dreaming of her steady.

Sat. Oct 22. Uncle John, Aunt Tina, Norb & his wife are here. Was out with Norb & his wife. Went & cancelled the freight shipment of our furniture.

Sun. 23. My first Sunday without her. Sat in the folk's seat. Went up to Father Wilkes & had a Mass ordered for Monday.

Mon. Oct 24. Mother, Dad & I went to Vi's Mass. I received & went to confession too. Got home, then Kenneth & I took out the cabinets & then I first saw that almost half was broke.

Tues. 25. Gerhard Roeric's Wedding. That was the wedding Vi said she'd attend regardless what happened. Kenneth & I went to the mass & then I took him up to Father Wilkes. Kenneth & I repaired as much as we could. Pain increasing in my back. Best night I had yet.

Wed. 26. Ann & Cyril here. First found her diary today. Pain awful this morning. Kept on getting worse so we went to Dr. Liebold's. Said its just bruised inside. Told me he couldn't have saved Vi either. Said it was an internal hemorrhage of the lung. I think my pain is mostly from bruising my kidney again. Oh God! What will I do without her. I just think she'll come down some morning with that friendly "Good Morning" like she always used to say.

Thurs. Oct 27. Weather Fair. Kidding Coli today & last night. No decent sleep. To Alex with my car. Left it at the Ford garage & came home with a '34 V8. Up to Kirland, Hoplin & the depot. Fell & hurt my back. Want $198.00 to boot. Mr. Hoplin says I should get at least $30.00 a month pension. Sent our stove & studio couch back. Terrible pain in my back. They want $50.00 to repair my car. I, Herb & Kenneth took over a 1.00 worth of products to Uncle Joe's, then over to Iggie's. Fat, Alfred, Ed & Melvin & all thought it was a bargain. Ethel & Frank here in the evening. My back is getting worse right along. God help me get well so I can quit dope, start working, forget my troubles, pay this car & earn money so she gets plenty masses.

Fri. 28. Warm. Mom & I to town & over to Aug. Korkowski. Got my check from Sears. Chris here, told me to have rings and a new clutch put in. Pat over to Fat shingling his house. Herb, I & Kenneth to Alex, tried to get the V-8 for 175.00, said he'd have to see the boss first. Chris took us home. Over at John Klimek's party, then went home.

Sat. 29. Beautiful weather. Slept till 10, then Chris came & Herb, I & Kenneth went to Alex. Again. Ford wants $200.00 for the V-8 '34 model with rings, clutch included. We went to the Olds. Garage & there we picked up a '35 Chev at $200.00 to boot plus a few other encumbrances. Installed heater & rear view mirror, got home around 5 o'clock. I think Chris will be plenty mad at me. Up to Art & Vern's for supper (pheasant), there till 10, gave them a ride & had to tell Vi's & my hardships. Honestly I feel a lot better now, after talking about her for a while again. Lots of pain in my back. Got a letter from Vi's Mom, Roers Sisters (Nuns) & the Upland Co.

Sun. 30. Nice weather, Herb bought .50 cents worth gas & Kenneth, Herb & I were out riding all afternoon. Up to where it happened (accident) twice. The three of us first alone and then we took Mary over there, too.

Mon. 31. Out selling with Kenneth, started where we started the first time. Stopped at Gordon's, got change. I have to talk & explain too much to do any real business. Got some SC 36.

NOVEMBER 1938

Tues. 1. ALL SAINTS DAY. Fair. To church, took Kenneth with me, read the mass of the dead, & two masses besides that. Herb & I to Alex., got the heater fixed. Up to Kirland, tried dirty work.

Wed. 2. ALL SOULS DAY. Fair. Went to church, read 3 masses, also visited Vi's grave yesterday & today. Pat & I to Alex. Relief office to Hoplin's told me to come back tomorrow.

Thurs. 3. Cold, wind. To the relief office. Paid Pa's insurance & light bill, got my tools for the car. Vern & I out retailing on the way home. Sold $4.15 in three hours. Flat tire, received the tire & tube.

Fri. 4. Cold, fear. Had to stay home on account of the relief inspector. Got drunk, God help me I shouldn't have done it but it's too late now God forgive me.

Sat. 5. Had to have Alfred pull out my car from a rut where Martin drove it down. We got home around three o'clock. We ran out of gas & also burned out the battery completely. Pat told me either get rid of the car or go myself. Told him I'd take the car & go myself too. To Alex. Got my model A battery & carburetor adjusted. For dinner at Lidy's, lunch &

supper at Ann's. Made arrangements with her to stay for & pay 10% from the profit, & also can get Harley for some money. Had to buy a tire & tube & got a used one from Joos. Jake put it on. Got him a $1.00 bottle Of cough syrup. Got a letter from Spiegel's. Ann & Cyril here in the evening. Why did I have to make a hog out of myself by over drinking?

Sun. 6. Fair. To church. Pat & Herb had it out for the last time, her last day yesterday. Bolted down the cabs in my car. Dad helped me do it. Mom & I up to Aunt Len's to see if we could get Bernie to work here again. I went up there in the Evening again. I don't favor it so much. Art, Vern, Mom, Dad & I over to frank & Ethel in the evening. Mary & Martin there also. My first night of alone sleeping since "it happened'. A long sleepless night. Two Rosaries before any sleep came at all, then restless yet.

Mon. 7. Fair weather. Froze oil in my car. Dad had to pull out & then push my car to get it started, cause I over flooded the motor then wore the battery down. Vern & I retailed from 10:30 to 12, sold $3.15. Then Mom, Vern & I to Alex. where the board met to decide how large a pension I should get. Decided $15 for 4 months. Visited Aunt Valaria. Got the ammeter adjusted & the throttle moved on my car. I returned my Spiegel order today, too, mind worse again & also wrote Bernie. Got home around 5 but went up to Vern's, there for supper. Got my cash worked up to $7.00 again. Got a card from Marvin Koeplin and also a letter from Vi's folks. Getting an abscess on my right hand. Passed a kidney stone, size of a small pea. Fourth one since the accident. Backache less. Started getting my order ready. Should have $25.00 to build my stock for a start again. Still can't figure why it had to happen. Oh! Lord! Help me forget everything. Maybe had it coming because of being crooked for a while. And why make a pig out of myself like Friday.

Tues. 8. Fair, cold. Mom & I to Parker's and paid Vi's casket, then told Liebold & Stensrud to put in their claim to the town board. Got home around 11, ate dinner & at 11:45 I started out retailing, first time alone since Vi left. My hand getting worse. Sold till 5, then got the chills & my arm started hurting with the hand. Sold $10.12. Why couldn't she stay & work with me. To think that I'm getting another abscess & she won't be there to take care of me like she did when I laid in bed those three weeks shortly after we were married, how she'd go & come running up those stairs every few minutes it seemed and ask "Is there anything I can do for my Raymond this time? Oh God! I'll go nuts thinking about "her" all the time. Now my hand starting again. With the pain feeling as though its ever cross into my left arm at the elbow & then noticing a kidney colic coming up to yet before the passing of another stone again. Lord Help me.

Wed. 9. Pain so dam bad in my hand that I didn't feel like getting up when Mom woke me. Want to mail my receipt to Spiegel & couldn't find the letter. Started for Brand to get a new one from the depot, had a flat, then thought of putting the letter in my car yesterday. Got the mail, an order to deliver tonic east of Garfield, did that. Over to Lidies for dinner & at Ann's for supper, Those two were quarreling. Got home at 7:30. Mary here sewing, Melvin got her in evening. Vern here too. No sleep last Night, hope I get some tonight.

Thurs. 10. Cool. Vern & I out selling and sold for $11.60. My hand still the same. It bothers so much at night, very little sleep. Art & Vern helped me get my records set. Just think, her & I going to bed at 7:30, I mean Vi & myself, almost every night, how we would say our prayers first, then as each other what had said the prayers for. After that, straighten out our record books, put our work aside & then start talking over how we met, fell, married, & still loved each other after being married thinking how everybody said that love would quit after that & both seeing how it grew instead of quitting like they said it would. How she used to tell me, "If somebody would unexpectedly come into our room, they wouldn't think there two in the bed the way we like to hug & kiss each other. Then after being through with our chores (hugging & kissing) as we called it, we would start planning about our future, which always seemed "bright" to us & the last few days more so then ever to think only a couple more weeks we'd be settled in a home of our own.

Fri. 11. Vern & I out selling again. Sold till 12, then had our lunch at Ann's & then didn't start again until 2:30 because I got so Darn sick, with a headache, sore eyes & vomiting steady. Sold for $9.35. Paid K.P. & also Fat today. Up to Ed's, getting Bud tomorrow, then up to Vern's, getting my order ready to send off. First one since it happened. Made me feel worse Than ever to think Vi isn't there to help suggest & figure out the things we need again. How her & I would sometimes do our ordering laying in bed. How Poik & his wife quarrel already & her & I never even had one real one yet (thought of that when I saw Poik's wife today up there trying to sell) Vern told me this evening how Vi told her to come up to our place after we'd moved, if she'd want to have a peaceful Sunday. I don't believe there's been a single nite since it happened, that I'd be able to get any sleep before 12:30 or even later. I'll go nuts thinking about it every nite after I go to bed. Feel sicker than heck & my hand hurt a little more tonite again.

Sat. 12. Snowed overnight & still is snowing. Picked up Bud but got scared out driving myself as I picked up Herb then went out. Over at Kate's for dinner. Kate showed the cabinet that Vi and I had in mind to buy from her when we moved. Mom & Dad made me feel awful bad when I came home. Felt sick all day again.

Sun 13. Cold, blowing. To church with Mom & Dad. This was our first Sunday Vi & I had planned to come home. She said yes, the first Sunday we want to be alone, & the next Sunday we go home for dinner. My hand hurts so much that I can hardly drive the car. If she were only here then I couldn't think of my hand steady. Am beginning to feel the pain I had right after the accident, (in my lung & chest) when I turn over in bed or when sitting to much & long or turning in a chair. Vern helped me straighten out Vi's records which her & I used to keep perfect up to date.

Mon. 14. 8 degrees below zero. Went to creamery, got Herb to help start my car. Him & I went to Alex & there they fixed the entire ignition system.

Tues. 15. Cold, snowed & blowed. Went to Brandon. Had Harvey Bolin look over car. Said same as the Alex fellows. Had dinner at Ann's, Then visited Lidy, Kate, Clara, Ethel & Mary. Supper over at Ethel's. Had to stay till 9:15 & had to tell them my "true story". Got stuck twice & finally ran out of gas at the last hill. Walked, forgot to drain the car so I took Dad's car & drove back. After draining it Dad's car ran out of gas so I left that stand & walked back home once more.

Wed. 16. Nice weather. To Alex with Art & Vern, drove home thin Brandon & picked up my truck shipment. Unpacked & checked it all that night.

Thurs. 17. Nice weather Picked up Halley & him & I went to Brandon & winterized my car. Out selling with him, first time in the afternoon, made out pretty good. I cleared $3.00 & he made 43 cents. Went home And got my books, started putting my amounts in order. Quite a bit fever, restless night with quite a bit of pain in my lumps.

Fri. 18. Fair. Out retailing, sold $10.05, not bad. Pain increasing in my arm & leg pretty fast.

Sat. 19. Nice weather again. Slept till 9 because I didn't get much sleep again in the nite. Had a terrible fever with the chills, last nite again. Harley & I ate dinner at Lidy's. While Bolin tried to find out the trouble with my car. Went to Alex and got my rods & main bearings tightened for $3.50. Got home around 10, after eating dinner & supper at Ethel's.

Sun. 20. Cool, snowed and blowed later again. Then the whole family over at Anna's for duct dinner and supper. Harley and I flushed my radiator, installed a thermostat & filled her up with gas & antifreeze. Also had a flat, had that fixed at Gene's. Terrible pain in both legs, besides some awful chills, & fever. I opened up this morning.

Mon. 21. Am getting pretty stiff from all the abscesses. Over at Harley's for dinner. Went out retailing at 3 o'clock. Sold 6.15 from 3 till 5, cleared $3.00, he .35 cents. Had supper at home, then H & I went over to Ethel's to sell a radio. Already had a different one, so H. fixed their old one. Met Bernie Buse at Ethel's. Stayed there till 11. They played cards.

Tues. 22. Cold. H & I drove home, got Ma to write a note then went to Alex. & got pills. Got back to Ann's at 3:30. Elreen & I finally finished up my account Books, which hadn't been taken care of since "She" left. Had to start where "she had balanced them, (who would have ever thought it would be her last time) Oct 17. How "she" said yet the day before it happened, "Come Orb let's get our books straight for once & always." Elreen & I also rearranged my new customers alphabetically. Don't believe I've gotten more than a half hour sleep for the last whole week.

Wed. 23. Fair, cold, snow again in eve. Mom, Dad, Art, Vern, Cappie & Ruddie over at Cyril's helping them butcher 5 pigs. H there, helped me start my car by pushing it up to his place. In at Harvey Bolins & had him put a bolt on the air filter. Another lump opened towards Evening. Needled 1 of them last night before going to sleep, bed. Went home this evening, had to take Ma to church tomorrow. Had in mind to needle 2 more lumps, but changed my mind, because I left the syringe lay in my car & didn't want to run out & unlock my car again. Lord! How I miss "her" when trying to stand this pain. Nobody to encourage me anymore, nobody left to suffer for. To think how she used to sooth the lumps by lightly tickling them after we'd get to bed, & also miss her shake my bed. If only I could at least write to her yet, or better yet talk to her. How can I help but wish that it only would be Our Lord's will to let me meet her soon, regardless of where she is & of how much I'd have to suffer before I'd go, if I could only love "him" & `her" like we loved them on this world. The way I feel now, I couldn't care what happened to me. I don't think I'd care if somebody'd give me life in prison, or I could still love & pray for her even better than I can now. 2:30 & I haven't said "our" Rosary yet, so with my imagination that "she" is still here in bed with me to hug & kiss each other Good Night like she always made me do it, I'll do it that way instead of only saying it like I did not since She's gone, GOOD NIGHT

Thurs. 24. Fair, cold. Mom & I to church. All over at Ed & Dots for dinner & supper, except Bob's, Clara, Lidy, Gene & Kate. Swell eats & also beer. I'm getting so shaky & nervous from lack of sleep. Just keep on think about `her"

steady & and getting so I don't know what to do with myself. Bawled all morning from pain & thinking she isn't there anymore. Asked for hypo & Mom can't find them again. Puts them some place then doesn't know where herself. Home alone with Mom & Dad in the evening. Not much to thank for on this

THANKSGIVING DAY

Fri. 25. Cold, snowed overnite again. I took my car & drove to Brandon to get pills. Had to get folks' consent first. Had dinner at Lidy's, lunch at Ethel's & no supper but midnite lunch at Aunt Lena's with Bernie. Had to take Justine over there & also take her back again, then Bernie went home with me, stayed overnite. Could get only 10 pills. Pain getting so dam severe that I'm really half-crazy at times. No sleep until 5:30. Showed Bernie my picture album & also let him read our "love" letters.

Sat. 26. Colder, snowed a little again. Opened up another 2 lumps again. Six that I opened altogether so far. Don't know what I'll do if this pain keeps up very much longer. At lease a pt. of pus in the last one I opened. Took Bernie home right after dinner. Him & I stayed there only a little while, then we visited over at Ethel's, then over at Mary's where we stayed for supper. Took Bernie home around 7:30, then I went and stayed at Ethel's until about 10 o'clock. I couldn't get myself undressed so I had to call Mom. She undressed me and also got me a pill for pain. Hardly any sleep again.

Sun. 27. Fair. Couldn't hardly go to church this morning so painful every lump was again. It'll never seem like a Sunday to me anymore since she's gone. To think how we'd be sitting at home after we'd moved, & now she's left me forever all alone with nobody that will ever care for me and love me the way "she" did. Mother's Birthday. Nobody here in the day except Vern. In the evening Lidy, Gene, Elnor, Cordon, Ann, Cyril, Ethel, Frank, Mary, Melvin, Art & Vern here. Brought the lunch along. Gene & Gordon left me some whiskey. Mom & I opened another lump after they all left. Worst pain I've had within the last 6 months. "She" helped needle that one before we were even married yet, & to think how good "She" was at it too right from the start.

Mon. 28. Nice day. Such terrible pain again, just can't help think & say things I shouldn't be saying. What would I do if Dear Mother wouldn't be here. Wouldn't keep on feeling so terribly bad about Vi leaving me but I'm so terribly afraid that she (Mother) won't live as long as Dad will. Then what will I do, left all alone here. Mom & I to Parker's, had to show Liebold my lumps before I got any pills. Pain so terrible that I had to wait for the hypo to work over at Elnor's. She took my side just as much as Moms when she told me taking so many pills again. I'm afraid I'll have to leave home pretty soon anyway, as much as I'd hate on account of Mother's sake alone. They'll never see into my side of it I'm afraid. Oh God, to think how hard it would be on Poor Mother. After all she' already done for me & then I should go & disappoint her like that. But I just can't stand going crazy from suffering such pain either. Lord Thy Will Be Done. Took 3 hypos & only got 1 1/2 out of it. Got a letter from Vi's Mother. Just couldn't help but cry for about an hour after reading it. Just seemed almost like getting the letter from Vi. Got another hypo at night from Mom.

Tues. 29. Awful nice day again. Lord what can I do but beg for pills with such terribly unbearable pain like I've got this morning. I know I did wrong again, but with only Love gone, Vi, the only girl I've ever loved and cared for in all my life, now gone for ever. I just didn't know what to do to forget her at least a little, but with such pain, I just can't help think of her all the time. I just don't care to live anymore & don't care what happens to me, although I feel just terribly terribly sorry for Poor Dear Old Mother after all she's done for me. Oh Lord! Help Mother & Dad see it my way at least when I have so many big lumps. And also help me so I won't get another habit again ever for Vi's sake if for nobody else's sake. Lord let Vi pray so I die a happy death like she did soon, before I cause my Dear Mother to much trouble, grief & worry. Around 7:45 my pain started getting worse & Mother & I went to town & got a pint. Took half of it then went to bed. Slept till 1, then I woke up from such terrible pain that felt as though somebody had shot into the lump. I think its from the whiskey. Mother gave me two pills for a hypo, but couldn't even lay still long enough to take that. Took 2 aspirins lst & about an hr. later I could first take the hypo.

Wed. 30. Nice weather again. Pain just like it was last nite. Took a hypo again at 8:30 & another one at 2, it slipped off so I took another one, then Mother & I needled a lump, opened it, least A pint of pus. Another 1/2 gr. H at 7:30. Took 3 1/2 gr. H during the last 24 hours. Uncle Aug here in P.M., Art & Vern in eve. & Al Schecher came in evening too. Dot here too PM. Dot says Theresa Klein isn't expected to live longer than a day or two. Isn't it just to hard to figure out, she who has them kids to look after has to go, & I can't go. Here where it would be better for me & for the rest. Lord, if it be Thy Will let me die, even if I'd have to suffer a lot, just so I could go & meet my "Beloved dear Violet" the girl that "loved" me & would do anything for me, as soon as possible.

DECEMBER 1938

Thurs. 1. Pain still the same yet. My bed just soaked in pus this morning. Took the last pill, then killed the half pint of whiskey still left. Pain got worse again after it worked out. In the afternoon Mom & I to Brandon, wanted to see Hoplin to find out if I couldn't get my medical fee paid. He wasn't home so we drove to Alex. to see the women. She made out an order right away & called up Kirland & told him to take me first. I really didn't even ask for it & she suggested it as soon as I told her how terrible pain I had. Kirland wrote out one prescription after another, took temperature, pulse, respiration, tested my blood, & took a specimen of my urine too. Got a tube of "phines". When Mother asked him how many I'd need, he said I'd have to know that & that Mom should be able to see & that it depends on how much pain. Got at least 4.00 worth of medicines besides the doctor's service fee. To think how nice Vi & I would have had it, because we would have got this all free besides all the groceries "we" would have needed if "we" wanted it. The only thing we really would have had to earn would have been our rent & they even pay that in some cases. Got my check from Spiegels $30.32 Must get it cashed so I can pay Father Wilkes, Joe Joos, & Upland Co. Pa and Al sawing wood at Art's.

Fri. 2. Drizzled, Mom & Dad helped butcher at Art & Vern's. I & Al went up there for dinner. Stayed till 4:30. Pain still the same, getting worse in my right leg. I didn't ask for any pills all day & then when I did ask for this evening Mom raised just as much hell as when I'd ask for 2 pill 3 times a day. God! How I miss my Dear Violet when I have to argue & quarrel for pills every time. If she only were here yet then we would have been moved & most of these lumps never would have come. I doubt if any would have come if she only could have lived. Haven't told anybody yet why these lumps are coming again, & I know for sure that they wouldn't have come if she only could have stayed with me & could have kept on take care of me so good like she always use to. Don't think I'll tell anybody or its too late now. Oh God! Is my pain ever severe tonight again Started putting on ice packs which stops the pain for a few minutes but looks like its getting unbearable now again. Honestly I can't even breathe any more. Oh Lord! How can I ever stand it & I just don't dare ask for any more pills either. She'd get a cat fit like Vi used to say, if I'd ask for any more, even when she saw & knew that almost half went to the dogs again of the one I did take. Oh God, if only my Vi were here to keep me company like she used to & Sooth the lump by rubbing it gently like she always did. Then I could try to forget yet, but this way its impossible without her. Left me forever.

Sat 3. Fair. Looks like snow. In bed till 6 towards evening. Dad & Mom to Osakis with Fred Gaddos trying to trade cows with him. They came home around 5:30 P.M. Made a trade paying $8.00 to boot. Needled another lump. Lucille here from 7 till 1:30 in the afternoon. Kept me some real company. Her and I looked through Vi's & my album. Showed her the poem I made up about Violet, & talked about Vi all during that time. Pain increasing in the evening again, was pretty good until now. Schecker to Alex. Had to take an extra hypo at nite. Believe it or not I could swear I didn't get a half hr. of sleep again, & the little while I did sleep I dreamt of her still living & that she was rubbing the abscess gently to sooth the pain & when I did wake up to find she wasn't there any more anyway I could have screamed at the top of my voice to find it all a dream after all. Honestly I just couldn't even get my breath, & that took me so long to get that my heart pounding & hurting which scared me so much that I called Mother & she brought me the extra hypo.

Sun 4. Cloudy again, I wanted to go to Mass, but Mom wouldn't let me go, so I read a Double Mass for Violet in bed, besides a lot of other prayers for "her". My first Mass I had to miss since I met my Dear Beloved Wife Vi over six months ago, and "she" didn't miss any from the time "she" started turning Catholic even before "we" were married. She could use "her missal" (I bought her a Missal just like mine the day before she was Baptized) just as good as I could. Took a 1/2 gr. Hypo in the morning before they went to church, but the lst one was a slip off again, but the 2nd one was a real hit though. Went over to Kate's for diner & supper. Vi had told me yet, "There we'll never dare go for a meal because she put up such a swell meal, which means we will have to do the same & that's something we won't be able to afford from the beginning". To think she never got a chance to even cook for me like she was planning every day for the last 2 weeks, just seems to tear my heart out of me. Why did she have to leave me forever so soon & let me alone to suffer in this world even more then ever. Never was I more able to bear the pain more easily then I could when & after I got to know & married to "her". The worst pain seemed only half as bad as it really was, when "she" was with me all the time. Oh God! If only it be His Will, let me suffer plenty, then let me join "hell' in heaven real soon. I will think if I can possibly make it I'm going to try & earn enough to have one read every month on the day that she died. And if I should make out real good later on, one Mass also on the 21st of each month the day she was buried on.

Mon. 5. Foggy & cloudy all day, fair. Pain still the same & very little sleep again last night again. No hypo during the night. Needled another lump, then opened it with the scissor that Vi always used to open my lumps quick for me, her manicure scissor. Still 3 more lumps coming yet. Never felt so downhearted, heartbroken & disgusted as I did today, in all my life & right in the morning too already. Got my lst pay check. If only my "Dearest Vi" were here to appreciate this check with me, but this way it don't even mean a thing to me except that I have a means of paying my debts with it, & have masses read for her off & on. Its not the check yet, but will get over for this order when signed & returned.

Tues. 6. Windy & snowed & blowed, also. Mom & Dad butchering over at Uncle. Aug. I took my car & went to see Rademaker. Gave me a 1/2 gr. Hypo & 2 pills beside. Stopped in at Bob's & was going to get a pint. Then Clara told me that Mom had forbid them to sell me one. Pa came in & got one for me. Killed 1/2 of that right away, couldn't eat any supper so I went to bed. Al & I talked till 10:30 then he went to his bed. I slept about 10 minutes then woke up around 1:30 with such terrific pain that I really thought this would be the last of me. Pat & Fat went to Brandon & got pills for me, got back at 4, took 1 1/2 gr. Hypo & at 6:30 I fell asleep. Slept till 9:30 this morning

Wed. 7. Snowed terrible heavy all day. Sold turkeys, $54.11 for 25. At 1:30 Mom & I went to Alex. Got my order endorsed & check cashed too. Up to Kirland, prescriptions for Novocain, Wrights Powder & Gauze. Said 3 3/4 hypos in 24 hrs. is too much. A grain & half in 24 hrs.

should be all needed for the worst pain. Got home at 6:15. Ate supper, took 1/2 gr. Hypo. Mom making sausage at Peero's. Went there with Art & Vern. Pa & I home alone. Vern helped me needle 2 lumps this morning. Vi's job something she'll never do for me again, & to think how good she was at it too, just as good if not better then myself, she was more steady at it than I was.

Thurs. 8. Immaculate Conception 2nd Mass I've got to miss. Never missed one while Vi & I were together except the time I was sick in bed 3 weeks of course & only missed 1 more then even. Just think, "she" would have been keeping house for me for over a month already, 38 days to be exact. Would have been our 6th day of obligation. I wonder what we would have done today, stay home again or if we would have gone home for dinner at Mothers. Well I guess she'll never get a chance to cook nor go home with me for dinner either. Ally & I to Parker's, I got a copy of the prescription for the sleeping pills. Over at Al Roers in the evening with Art and Vern. Broke my syringe tonight. My first visit I made without Violet. It didn't and I guess it won't ever seem like visiting without my "Sweet Violet" Called "her" Sweet Violet reminds me of how she always used to call me My Dear Daddy, Pappa, or Raymond mostly.

Fri. 9. Fair. Another lump opened this morning "our" little comfort pillow all full of pus. Al slept with me again. Pain plenty bad yet, & last night I thought I just couldn't stand it. Such a high temp. I had. This morning Pa right away said he could see it on me & Ma said the same. The high fever does that every time, that's why I didn't want to go there. Lord help me! It just seems like I was an animal around here the way I'm being treated this morning. When I told Pa that Kirland said when lumps come like this I can take 3 1/2 gr. hypos in a day then he told me yes, all right, if you don't ask for more than that, you'll never hear me scold, now I didn't ask for more & this morning & still he's raising hell again now & Mom want me to get our of bed & I can't on account of the hypo slipping off & such pain. How I wish she were only here so we could be moved like we planned or that I could be with her where she is now which would be better for me yet. Just happened to think of our Wedding Day when my "Sweet Little Wife" & I drove over to Aunt Lena's to get some fresh flowers for the eve., then we drove the old road going home & stopped in that little hollow & there had our 1st marriage relation (intercourse) then got home & I went upstairs with her in our room & helped her fix the straps which busted during the day, on her slip or petticoat, how we both had to blush, feel foolish first then both laugh like crazy. And all the fun & laughing we both did when she'd give me a bath every Saturday. night & take one herself almost every night, then go at our Shade+Tare when we'd get into bed. Honestly, we'd both laugh till our stomachs would hurt sometimes, when she'd tell me to let her count the inches, which was the thing that thrilled her most. Yes! I guess them days are gone forever. "She's" got her good place of eternal Rest & Joy, but what I've got left & coming yet & what this world holds for me yet, I'm afraid won't be any thing good. Lord let it be Thy Will to let me suffer, die, & then meet & join & enjoy myself with her, my "dearest Violet", as soon as possible, real soon, like we both met, loved, joined & enjoyed ourselves on this world before this all happened. Going to bed every night, alone, with nobody to undress me quickly on these cold nites. No one to talk to, plan, with, plan & work for, she isn't here to pray with me anymore, to think she'll never tell me like she always used to, Hug & Kiss me my dear Raymond, & to think she'll never ask me to Hug, Kiss & tell Goodnight like she'd always made me do, & I'd always tell "her" yet that I was a "bear" not a "dear" when she'd say "My Dear Raymond", or My Dear Daddy or

Pappa. To think I can't even talk or worse yet, not even write to "her", never, really stops my breath, makes my heart seem to feel & making me think of going insane, feeling as though I've just got to scream at the top of my voice, when thinking of "her" & of it all at times. Ed Loeffler had to pull Mom & I into town when we went to Alex. This morning or noon. Pipe line clogged. Up to Kirland's, got a new syringe, needles, thermometer, sleeping caps & phines also. My right ankle swollen & so painful that I just don't know what to think or do.

Sat. 10. Beautiful weather again. Pain not quite so bad this morning. A 1/4 gr. hypo in AM. And 1 1/2 gr. in the eve. 15 pills left from the Alex. Tube. This evening the pain is so severe again, that I could hardly make the steps to go to bed. Felt so darn "blue" today, think of me having to spend the Xmas alone without "her" how she had told me yet, that she was going to get me some pajamas for this Xmas & a carton cigarettes for both of us how I had planed to get her a Satin house coat that she could wear around the house as a maternity coat how she told me yet that she'd want to sew all winter making clothes for the "Baby-to-Be" or Raymond Jr. as she always called it now she's gone and left me alone to keep on thinking of all our plans that we never got a chance to see or put through & carry them out. Had the most Beautiful Dream I've ever had since happened about her & I being together in bed once more, loving each other up again just like we really used to, last night, really, I felt so god & Happy. If I could only dream of her like that every night, it would help so much. God! How my R. ankle & lumps hurt now since I'm in bed this evening.

Sun 11. Fair, snowed little. I had to miss another Mass again. I don't believe I got an hour of sleep last night again. Took 2 sleeping caps at 2:30 & a 1/2 gr. hypo at 6:30. A 1/2 g slip off today, only 7 pills left. Was over at Father Wilkes, paid him & Joos socked me $18.00 for Mass & Grave digging, outrageous I think. Over at Alfred's for a visit with Herb. Quite a lot of pain this evening again. Won't dare to ask for hypos tomorrow. Hope it won't pain so very much.

Mon. 12. Nice weather again. Fair nights rest again for a change. Not much pain till around 3:30 then the lump on my R leg started hurting terrible. Was going to get a pint. Then Ma said I should wait till Pa came home, said she thought he'd give me a 1/2 gr. hypo so I could needle & freeze it. Tried out my freezing liquid on healthy flesh first, then Ma & I froze & needled the lump. It sure works fine. When I froze good flesh first, I froze it so good that I could pinch it, I stuck a needle in it & scratched it so hard that it bled & I couldn't feel it a bit. To think her & I wouldn't ever had to spend a cent on account of the lumps except a little for pills for the pain, which wouldn't have been much because she wouldn't give any more than just so much or so many because she could tell pretty dam close how bad my pain really was. "She" always told me she could tell how bad the pain was be sleeping with, said I would breathe so uneven, moan a little, & that I'd be so restless & would be so restless and rub my leg against her stomach or back just steady. Pain never seemed so bad & wasn't so hard to bear either with "she" to keep company & help keep my mind off of the pain. And then we'd always have so much to talk about & plan about that I'd never really think of or feel pain, & when it did hurt so much that I'd start complaining, she'd grab me, hug & kiss me & then tell me, "It doesn't matter My Dear Raymond, just so we still have each other to "hug" "love" & "kiss" & keep in mind, now you can always have a "shade-tare" from me anytime you want it, even when you're sick in bed now", & that would make me forget the worst pains. Now, to think she was the one that left me, left me forever, & right at a time when I need her consoling words & actions so bad, more then I ever needed her before. Nobody will ever be able to do for me what she has been doing for me since the time we fell in "love", nobody will ever be able to take "her" place, not even my kind, Dear Old Mother. How can I ever keep on living without her. I know Mom loves me lots, but it isn't the same, true "love" that My Dearest Vi had for me, and I know I'll never "love anybody like I did her either.

Tues. 13. Fair. Terrible pain in the lump I needled last night. Took a 1/2 gr. hypo this morning. 1 slip off & a 1/4 gr. this evening last one too. Was going to see Hatley & when I got to the car the switch had been on since last Sunday. Put the battery on the windcharger, also added water. Wrote a letter to Ray Murray telling him all about myself & My Dearest Violet.

Wed. 14. Cold. My battery charged up pretty good overnight. Al pulled me out of the yard then the car started already & then I drove over to Ann's, there overnite. Harley & I home with the kids while they were to Gene's Birthday Party. Had to tell Harley & Elreen my enjoyment of married life, giving them both the "lowdown" of it & waning them of the treachery of the present day way of young youth. Am I weakening again? I guess so.

Thurs. 15. Nice day again. Opened the abscess this AM that Mom & I froze & then needled. Leg felt so fine that I have in mind to go out retailing tomorrow. In the P.M. my leg (from knee down) started hurting so much that I really was scared. Am getting another 2 lumps, maybe 3. Leg felt as if paralyzed. Ann had aluminum cooking demonstration this evening and swell supper at 7:30 & breakfast at 8:15. Felt sorry I didn't go home on account of the terrible pain as I'm afraid I might start hollering in my sleep because that usually happens when pain is severe. Taking only sleeping cap. Had a pony of Beer at Party also. Now I understand why Vi wanted a "Dutch oven". She used to tell me it would save on fuel & groceries & I believe it now after seeing it demonstrated. Used to tell me, "she'd" have only one kettle to wash, because she could cook an entire dinner on it for at least 3 or 4 people, & that I wouldn't need to help do dishes then. Hardly no sleep again. Lord why couldn't she have stayed at least long enough to have tried keeping house for me.

Fri. 16. Cold, snowed, blowed. At Lidy's, Ethel's (Vern, not home) then went home and I can't go out & sell anyway with 2 lumps again. Cyril had to push my car to start it, even a new coil & distributor and rotor that I bought Wed. for it, it wouldn't start because of a weak battery. Weakening? And how. If "she" were only here, I could easily "straighten out", & then "Brace up", but not alone & without her help. Lord if they could only understand me.

Sat. 17. Fair, cloudy, windy Home in A.M. to see how she'd start when put in the shed. First half turn she went off. To town in P.M. to cards for Harley's introduction to be typed on but couldn't get them in town. Over at Mal's, but she wasn't home so I visited Ethel's again, after getting back from the "sad scene of the accident" where I had to go to get over my terribly lonely blue spell again that I had today. Weakening more every day the way it looks. At Ethel's for supper again, and then till 8. Got home at 9 o'clock, every-bpdy in bed except Dad. Talked over Dear Violet's short past in our lives. And to tell him how "Her" & I met, fell in love, married, & planned our future, all in vain. Really felt better after telling him this all. More pain in leg again.

Sun 18. Fair. Mom and I both home from a church. A mass for my dear Violet Thursday by Ethel. Pain in my lumps and so I took the sleep caps, then was so darn tired that I didn't go to Elnor's for supper.

Mon. 19. Fair. Over at Harley's to get him lined up to go out alone. Another one of those "blue spells" again. Wonder what my Vi would think if she knew. Pain increasing in abscesses.

Tues. 20. Fair, blowed, snowed & cold. Harley & I out selling. Sold S12.05. Paid Pa & repaid some more debts. Got my lst S15.00 check today. Lord how blue I feel to think how nice Vi & I could have had. No doctor or druggist bills and God knows what they would've all furnished for why couldn't we have a chance at life like all the rest get. Why must I have all this hard luck! Guess it's all my fault.

Wed. 21. Fair. Harley took me home then went out selling alone for the first time. Mom and I to Alex to get pills. Fixed the Christmas tree lights, then Vern, Mom and I trimmed the tree. Reminds me of her some more, how she told me we'd send for a snow-covered artificial tree about 3 ft. high, & decorate with one of those dry cell Flicker light sets we saw in Alex the last time she and I did any shopping (the time we got pills and went to the show) my last and only wish I'd like to have that is Die a Happy Death like she did as soon as possible and meet her wherever she is. Even if I'll have to suffer a lot yet before I had die just so I could be together with "her". Won't seem like Christmas to me without "her" here with me. I asked her yet what we'd do Christmas Eve, when she told me she had been to a Christmas midnight Mass before already & that she thought it was awful beautiful she told me we'd find out if the folks would stay up & if they would, then we'd go there & then receive & go to Millerville church, and if the folks wouldn't stay up then we'd spend Christmas Eve with Aaron and Cyril, and now to think I've got to spend it alone without "her'. Lord! How I hope this will be my last one alone here.

Thurs. 22. Snowed & blowed today. Mother & I to the Mass Ethel had read for my dear "Vi". Went to Father Wilkes and ordered another mass for her Christmas morning at 7:30, the only kind of present I'll ever be able to give "her" yet. How I wish she could have lived at least till after Xmas & New Year so we could have given each other gifts like we had planned. What a merry & happy Xmas that would have been. How terribly I missed her today when I got such an awful attack of kidney colic at 4:30 this afternoon that I couldn't even take a hypo anymore & had to get Vern to help me take it. About 2 weeks before it happened, I got an attack too & she would give me the hypo then. Took a 1/2 gr. at 4:30 & one at 10:30 again.

Fri. 23. Nice weather today. Pain letting up a little. Two 1/2 gr. hypos today again. Mom & Al to confession already. Harley quit, not enough in it, bought the car back. In the evening around 10:45 I had to vomit & after that I got another attack. Terrible pain, took another 1/2 gr. hypo, at 1 the stone passed from kidney to bladder.

Sat. 24. Snowed, fair. Pain gone from kidney stones. To town in the forenoon. Around 9:30 the stone started coming out. Over at Bob's, then road out to Paul Klimek's, settled up with them for helping us out the day of the accident, by giving her a bottle of lemon extract. In the afternoon I was over at Mal's till 4:15, then to confession, then went & got my concertina from Ann's, & for supper over at Ethel's there till 9:15. Folks mad because I didn't come home sooner. Art & Vern here overnight.

Sun 25. CHRISTMAS, All of us, and Vern, to midnight Mass and received. Weather cold, stormed. All home except Ciene's & Gordon's. Three carton of cigarettes from Mom & Dad. I got a scarf, shirt, 3 pairs of silk socks and two packs of Philip Morris cigarettes. Didn't go to another

Mass, I had one read for Violet at the lst high mass because the stone bothered too much. Felt tough all day. Lord how I hope this will be my last Xmas with out "her". Pain increased so much that I had to take a 1/2 gr. hypo, then took 2 crocheting hooks & Butts & I tried to take out the stone. Its so dam big that I know for sure I'll never get it crushed.

Mon. 26. Snowing & storming again. Couldn't even pass last night without pushing the stone back first every hour. Don't believe I slept an hour and 1/2 all last night. Oh God! How I wish My Sweet Dear Violet were only here yet, then we'd be moved & her & I would live by the highway & we could go the a Dr. whenever I'd want to & to know we get on top. To think we would have come home yesterday like the rest & how I would have enjoyed it being about to do like she always used to say, "You & I'll show the rest we can make our own living & that we can take of ourselves just as well as they can". I'll show them I can take just as good a care of you as they ever gave you & that I won't get tired of it & give up like they always said I would." How she'd always say "It doesn't matter my dear Raymond, just so we have each other, to hug, Kiss & love like we can & do now all the time." Before we were married, when everybody was against us, when they sent her away that morning, then I told her yes, if they won't let us get married & if we can't have each other, I'll not want to live & I'll give up but not the way you or they think suicide. How she used to tell me, "Ray don' think of or try to do anything foolish like suicide. We'll keep on trying until we die in the attempt & that time I was so far gone, from dope, that I just didn't care to live, until I met "her", and now had to started again because she left me here, alone to grieve and cry & run myself down, weaken so much that lumps are coming all over, she left me alone to lug the sample case around by myself & weaken still more, with the lumps comes pain, then me asking for pills, then catch "hell" so I get half crazy at times. Then some of the rest go against me, & who wouldn't think of doing what she call "foolish". If I only knew that I wouldn't have long to live, then I'd go, leave them so I'm out of there way, where I wouldn't have to bother them, some place where I'd be out of everybody's way. How I wish I could only have gone with "her", or that I could leave here, go somewhere where I could be alone with my only true "friend" left. Why did we have to be parted? Its hard enough to bare, just to think she's gone, but then Mother has to go tell me yet that she can be lucky she's gone, & things that mean as much as to say I wasn't worth having her or that she was to good for me in other words I am, was, & always will be, an absolute, good for nothing bum or hobo. Who would still care to live yet after hearing that or rather that same story every time I get a pain & ask for pills. And who'd suffer any more than he has to after having over 7 years of living "hell" like I've been having. My only wishes The Lord's Will to suffer, die & then meet & be together with "her" within the near future & if not that then to be able to leave "home", & go somewhere far away where nobody would find out. Well, guess I'll have to live in hopes once more like my dear Vi & I had to before we finally got married. At 2:15 Pa, Art & I left for Alex to go to Dr. K. but went as far as Brandon, called him up, he wasn't home. We went back home again. We got stuck & had to cut Ed's wire to get through. Storming all day. 8 degrees below zero. Got another 1/4 gr. hypo before I went to bed yet. Fourth night of hardly no sleep.

Tues. 27. 22 degrees below zero. WE WOULD HAVE BEEN MARRIED 6 MONTHS TODAY IF SHE WOULD HAVE LIVED YET. Didn't pass since last. One 1/4 gr. hypo this morning & that slipped off yet. Why can't she be here to go to the Dr. with me today. To Alex in the afternoon with Mom, Art & Vern, over to Kirland's. He could crush the stone so we have to come back tomorrow & have Haskel do it. Got a tub of pills, 1/8 gr. tablets. Have to push the stone back every time I pass. Six 1/8 gr. tabs all day, & there's 16 left in the emergency tube.

Wed. 28. Called. 5 tabs this morning but 3 melted in Butts hand. Old Man told me this morning that he found out I had been to Fergus quite a few times to get pills, but that Bill S. Said I only got pills once from there. Mom & I quarreled too, she told me as though Vi must have been a pretty good liar if she could lie to them when they knew for sure it was so about the quarrel one dance. Told her she should leave Vi out of it, and that I quit dope this last spring on account of Vi & that I started taking it again this fall because she left me. How I wish I could avoid these quarrels with Dear Old Mom, really feel sorry for her. Called up Kirland in the afternoon, told us Haskel wasn't home yet, so we're not going to Alex today after all. Art & Vern here playing cards this eve. Listened to Gang Busters lst time since she & I listened before it happened.

Thurs. 29. 30 below zero, stormed. To Doc Haskel with Ed, Dot, kids & Mom. Had to take ether in order to have the stone removed. Nobody watched it, I know if my Dear Violet were still here she would have watched while they operated. Had to open the penes to get out the stone. And do I ever feel tough from the ether & is the penes ever sore now. Got home at 3:45. Ed drove with his car. Got the statement from Upland & Co today, 8.14 balance left.

Fri. 30. Cold, 22 below zero. Penes swollen so bad this morning that I can't pass any yet. Took 1/2 gr. hypo this morning. Sent off a New Year card to Norb & Lilly. I didn't know that they opened the penis so far that they had to put in one stitch until last night when I went to bed, The

"Grouch" claims I took his bottle of phines away a make believe, that's all it is. Frank Daas Family here in evening. Took 3 caps for pain & sleep this eve.

Sat. 31. Fair. Old Man & I to Alex. I to Doc's. Got pills and put on salve and told me another stone was coming & that I should come back Tues. or Wed. Tried to pull out my car to start it, saw I had a flat tire. At 2:30 A.M. I felt another kidney stone attack coming on. A New Years card from "Her" folks & a letter from Bernie. 12 1/8 tab today. 1 slip off though. Not a wink of sleep till 2:30 Should of had a Mass read for me Dearest Violet for tomorrow to make it a Happy New Year for her at least if not for myself.

JANUARY 1939

HAPPY NEW YEAR EVERYBODY

Sun. 1. Although I'll never have another happy new year like I had last year, the days I "met', falling in love", "married" my Dear Violet", I'd wish the rest one like that & just live in "hopes" that this will be my last, sad as it'll be to think I'll have to keep on living with out "her", my salvation, like it seemed. And now for my resolution For "her" honor & my Dear Mother If Dad & Mother agree with me. Dad is to give me 1 1/2 gr. H. today yet, 1 morning, 1 evening, Then for me not to positively take any more dope unless absolutely necessary for severe pain & then for me to quit taking it as soon as at all possible But if craving should bother a lot, then Dad is to give me 4 1/8 gr. tabs Mom & probably 2 1/8 gr. tabs Tues. but positively none thereafter unless absolutely necessary. Will go to Mass tomorrow morning to pray &ask Our Lord & ask Violet to pray for me, that I'll have the strength to carry out this Resolution. To get away from the craving (if any) I'll take the sleeping caps & Dad is not to get mad at me for taking the caps or if I should happen to get "tight" occasionally. This Resolution made at the stroke of midnight or in other words at the lst minute of the new year. Let's hope this meets both Dad & Dear Old Mothers

Approval. Got ahead in wishing all 3 a Happy New Year, then told them about my Resolution O.K. with them. I didn't go to church on account of backache. Dad & I talked over "our" (my dear Vi & my) happy life. Told I had a wife like very few in Millerville have a woman to be proud of & that compared in everything, looks, goodhearted, kind, religious and that loved me & thought the world of me, she could be compared with anybody anywhere he said & I know its true too. What a sad instead of happy year it will be for me without My dear sweet little wife, Vi, the only women I ever cared for & loved the way I did love her. To think we "two" would have been married 6 months now if she only could have loved, moved for ourselves "she" having "her" wish to keep house & cook for me like "she" wanted to. Would have now & been together with "her" now 8 month had she live now we're parted forever I can almost say for sure. How I only hope that I won't have to spend much of this here, alone & without "her". Art & Vern here for dinner. Mom, Vern & I over to Ethel's in afternoon. Art, Vern, Mary, Melvin here in eve. Not a wink of sleep until 3:15, just had to get the "blues" when I saw our Wedding Picture. To think how Happy we "both" were that day, & now to go to bed (in bed were "she" & I used to spend so many happy hours also) without "her" every night, & know "she's" not here anymore just doesn't see possible. It just seems as though it can't be true & still I know it is.

Mon. 2. Fair. Put the heel on Vi's shoe's. Mary wants them. Fastened the heel once before for "Violet" when she still lived, also soled them for "her" but she'll wear them no more. Al & I started my car & fixed a flat. Another stone in the end of my Penes. One 5/8 gr. H. 5 tabs in all today, 16 yesterday, but had two slip offs, 33 tabs from this last box, 7 only left. Al to Millerville dance, Mom & Dad & I to Vern's. Played whist & got a dam good lunch. Home at 10. Can't Pass any water yet.

Tues. 3. Fair. Took a H. 3 tabs then took out the stone, at 2:15 I took 2 more tabs. Al cleaned out my starter on the car, only 2 jinks to start the car today. Cleaned out Vi's cosmetic drawer & rearranged the things like "she" used to keep them.

Wed. 4. Mom went quilting over to Ann's. In the afternoon it started snowing & didn't quit until there was about a foot. Back started hurting around 10 in the A.M. Dad went to get the quilters & I was going home, lost a chain so they had to push me instead. Anti freeze boiled out again too. Bought a boot. In the evening around 11:30 I started getting another attack. Had taken two caps, but didn't help so I had to get 2 tabs. Got a letter from "her" Mom. Sad again.

Thurs. 5. Fair. blowing a little. Pain not quite so bad when I woke up but now its getting worse again, laying on a hot water bottle all night and now too. Got a terrible kidney attack around 4:30 P.M. again & the "old man" made a dam fool out of me just like he did this summer the time "she" cried so much when Dad wouldn't get me any pill for the pain from the 3 lumps I had & Butts & I went to sleep in the barn because he had bawled me out so much because I moaned. Vi cried something awful when I left her to sleep in the barn. Said he was childish & was a man without a heart or a heart of stone. Told me she wouldn't wish anybody hard luck but then she would wish him pain like I had for a couple days though. Drank lemon extract & took caps for the pain.

Fri. 6. Fair. Still the same backache. Dad wouldn't take Mom to Uncle Harry so she started walking to Ed's to go with him. When Dad & Al went milking. I took Dad's car & followed her & picked her up then got stuck by the sand pit Mom walked to Ed's & I walked to Cichy's and got Frank to shovel & Ed came & pushed with his car. Dad came walking as far as Al's road. Both went home & Ed followed Dad. Al to Klimek's. Got another attack and took some more ext. & caps for pain. Al had to fry me 2 eggs. They got home at 1:30.

Sat. 7. Fair. Same backache yet. Got a pill in evening and one slip. Had chills all day & evening.

Sun. 8. Beautiful day, thawed. Got another attack this morning. At 10:30 I took a 1/2 gr. hypo then took out another stone. In evening I took 1/4. gr. then took out another one & I think there must be another one there yet. Mom, Dad & I over to Klein's with Ed. The 1st outside visit that I've got anywhere near to enjoyment without Vi. Delores Cichy was there & she & I talked over the fun Vi & I had the night at Alex when I got home at 7:30 in morning.

Mon. 9. Rained all night & today. To Alex with Ed. Up to Haskel. He took the whole history of my case about dope & all. I really feel relieved Because the doctor admitted that morphine is the only thing to take to relieve the pain from the attacks. He gave me a receipt for dope & a medicine. If only the rest knew & understood like Violet did.

Tues. 10. Fair. Had our road opened yesterday by the snowplow. Same old backache again today.

Wed. 11. Fair. Al & I went to look for the chain I lost. Didn't find it. Bought a new battery from Jack. Art & Vern here Pulled my car to start it. Gas line blocks.

Thurs. 12. Nice day. Another stone coming again. Took 2 1/2 g. hypos so I could try get the stone out. Got one out but there's still one left. Over at Frank Daas in evening, Kleins there too. Al went home to his folks, said he would come to Daas to but he didn't show.

Fri. 13. Fair. Took another 1/4 gr. hypo to try get 2nd stone out but couldn't do it. Al didn't come home. Told the people in town he quit. Took his clothes last night while we were visiting. Finally got the stone out when I took another 1/2 gr. hypo, this morning. In the afternoon I told Mom, now I should be able to quit dope cause I haven't the slightest pain & after supper while milking I got the "Blues" with pain like a shot, terrific pain took a 1/2 gr. shot for that again. Art & Vern here for dinner & evening.

Sat. 14. Weather, fair and cloudy. Took a 1/2 gr. hypo then took out the last stone. Hope my plan will come through once & for always today. God help me win, for the last time. Heard the 6 Fat Dutchmen play over WNAX. To town, Herb & I to Junowoski and got him some money. For supper over to Tina's. Leo Wagner found my chain & he's got it Herb told me. My car still doesn't work the way it should. The battery goes down so dam quick all the time. Home at 6:30.

Sun. 15. Weather fair, colder, All to the lst Mass. First Sun I was to church this year. Art & Vern here for diner. Ed & Dot here in afternoon. Dot asked me to join their orchestra. Fat drums, Wilbur & Leo Hophner violin & sax, Dot on piano & I on the concertina. I had in mind to start under my own hook with Vern as the feature. Vern & I to Melvin's then to Alex. Show with them. Rob. Taylor, Florence Rice, Wallace Berry in "Stand Up & Fight". Ethel, Frank, Clarence & Lil here in evening

Mon. 16. Fair, cold. To town, but another distributor rotor then to Alex. Got some St. Caps Pill (bj) 1 dozen. Saw Pierce Lapman at the Berglunds Cafe. Visited Rita, gave her the tinted photo I had of Vi, and she gave me a little snapshot & is going to give me a couple others that she & Vi took in Hartland, just before they came to Millerville, that Vi never got to see even. Had supper at Kate's, picked up Vern & got home at 6:30. Art & I fried ourselves each 2 eggs before they went home yet.

Tues. 17. Snowed a little all day. Upland announced their coffee & paint prices Sat. Frank Klimek's first work day today. Came last night when all were in bed already. Sold our turkeys to Sam Fruth' s today. Made 8 new concertina keys, tore 2 off then glued 11 on, took both ends off to fix the reeds on 1 side & a key that leaked on the other side, made the bellows airtight & cut a strap to make myself a new style harness to play while standing & also better playing when sitting. Al set to get going. So what.

Wed. 18. Will finish my newly patterned concertina harness today. Hope they get started practicing with the orchestra pretty darn quick or else I'll start my gang like I had planned. Wrote a letter to Violet's Mother today. Bought 4 snaps for the harness, but couldn't finish it--strap too thick. My car caught fire when the muffler busted. Got my check today $15.00. In town all forenoon today. Ed Klimek, Kline's, Ed's & Art & Vern here. 2 1/4 gr. tabs to try & get a stone out again. Lord why can't Vi be here to help me forget & to help plan how to use the check best.

Thurs. 19. Fair weather today. Dad pulled my car out & tried to start it. She started right away so I left for Millerville right away. Stopped at Jake's & said told him I'd pay him tomorrow. Then to Brandon, got the check cashed & then I went over to Lidy's a while. Overnight at Ann.

Fri. 20. Fair weather again. Still over at Ann yet. In the evening I had to tell them about my self when I'd look & find the pills. The 3 of us all were up till 1:30. Not much doing in the day tine. Cyril & I drove to Millerville to pay Jake in the evening Then over to Bob's too, then home.

Sat. 21. Stormed. Had in mind to go home. Still over at Ann's. Called Mom & she said roads are tough, and not much to do. To Brandon & we put on a tail light. Pretty lonesome too. How I wish I could get home. Thinking of violet all the time. I just can't forget her, & who ever could forget a good woman like she was.

Sun 22. Stormed. Elreen & I made ice cream. Ann & the rest were to church but there wasn't any. So they were all home all day again, wishing I could go home. Got the Blues terribly in evening. I home alone in evening with the kids.

Mon. 23. Fair. Ann, Cyril & I to Cappie's this evening. Harley & I out to Evansville. Got 10 pills. Burned out a connecting rod between there & Brandon. Elreen to show in Alex with Harley, home before we were.

Tues. 24. Stormed. How I wish I could go home. Dad's 66 Birthday. Cyril & I over at Cappies. Called up from here but the roads are pretty tough. All went to bed early this evening. We didn't go at all. Ann & I argued.

Wed. 25. Stormed. Slept till Ann woke me. Ann & I over at Dot's quilting. How I wish I hadn't come home. Right away hell to pay when I came home. Art came & got Vern & Mule. To bed early. Lots pain in the lump coming. Hardly no sleep.

Thurs. 26. Cold. Still more hell to pay, this morning early. Best I can do though. Oh God! Why couldn't have my dear Violet have stayed with me, and she & I moved by ourselves like we had planned. What a nice living we would have had, she to hug & kiss & love me like she always did & I her. Them were the days & had something to live & work for. Got my invoice. No sleep as usual.

Fri. 27. Not so cold as yesterday. I wonder what today holds for me. God what a dream I had of Vi last night, so beautiful that I called Mom in my sleep when I dreamt she had come to open a lump for me, then to wake up & find it all a dream I just wonder how much quarreling I'll have to do today. Just another day without my Dear Sweet Violet. To town, got drunk, to Alex. Got pills, got an attack from a jar coming home. Got my order. Bluest day since 27 of Dec.

Sat. 28. Nice weather today. Still quite a backache this morning yet although the stone is almost through. Around 6 this evening I got it out after taking a hypo. 6 tabs gone, 2 slip offs, 14 left. Still had the "Blues" like I had yesterday. Seems as though I miss Violet more everyday instead of forgetting slowly & getting over the grief. I know I'll never get over it nor forget that sad day when she died. Never will forget those words, "Ray, I'm dying. Hug & Kiss me for the last time."

Sun 29. Cold. Art, Vern & Frank to church with the team. Frank tite when he came home. Took out 7 stones during the last 3 weeks. Finished the new price list today, prices that Vi suggested. Frank & I shook dice & also played cards & a little on the concertina. Uncle Joe, Aunt Tillie, Florian, Al & Berga here with sled in the evening. Played cards, I & Florian kept company. Auntie bought .50 cents pepper extract. Settled up thrashing bills. Talked over the road building.

Mon. 30. Fair. Nice weather. Frank & Dad to town with the young team. Both up to Art's helped him skin his horse that he shot today. Took out 2 more stones. Only 6 tabs left. Wrote a letter to Ford Motor Co. Vi's mother, & the Upland too. Another SAD DAY for me today. Around 8:30 this morning I noticed that I had lost Vi's wedding ring. Looked everywhere but couldn't find it. Am sure I had it on last night eating lunch yet.

Tues. 31. Weather. Sleet, colder. Dady & Mom butchering at Ed's. Made a different harness for the concertina, typed last years records of products purchased. Made a hypo water container. Have to go to Alex. To get the Relief Receipt notarized. Frank & I had to "batch" it today. I found my mortgage from my car that I had lost. Got the syringe & 36 S.C. I sent for Sat. today. Told Mom Vi's death bed talk, only some of it, though. About the first thing she said was, "Ray, I'm dying, I'm pinned under the car & can't crawl away". And then when we got her into Paul Klimek's house she said to me. "Oh Ray! I'm afraid I can't stand it until the Priest comes." Then no more was said until alone with her in the hospital, about dying. "Ray, I'm afraid I can't make it, & guess I'll have to leave you soon, but Ray, you know I always loved you, don't you? I've at least lived long enough to show Mother, Dad, the rest of your family & all the people that I was sincere in my love for you, and that I wasn't just a go-getter, just another finicky lover or a "whore", after your money like they all said, but that I married you because I loved you, & to make life happy for both of us. How I wish your Mother were here, so I could tell her all this, tell her I was sorry that I caused her all this trouble, but that I couldn't help it because I loved you too much to give you up easy."

FEBRUARY 1939

Wed. 1. Stormed & snowed terrible. Was kind of scared a while when I couldn't get the dam kidney stone out. Was supposed to go to Alex with Ed but now nobody possibly could go. Mailman didn't come today either, first time. Another stone coming in eve.

Thurs. 2. Storming again, cold. Nothing to do. Playing cards, shaking dice, listening to the radio. Fixed the lights yesterday, loose connection.

Fri. 3. Fair. To town with the sled. Herb & I to Alex. with Jack Hagen. Went home with John Pishkie. Got the order notarized at the court house. Herb & I bought Oj tabs. Paid Sygmund $5.00. P & Frank got me from the crossing where Fat brought me with his car.

Sat. 4. Fair. Frank Daas here last, played cards till 10:30 then ate lunch talked till 12:30.

Sun 5. Nice day. Got a letter from Mrs. Prestegard yesterday. Frank, Mom & I to church with the sled. Told Herb to get the car fixed & I took my stock home from Ed's. Checked the order, something "she" always used to do with me. Packed the sample case. Vern here. Played cards. Mom took a sleeping cap last night. Last FEEN (phine) today. How terribly lonesome the Sunday afternoons are since "She's" gone, it don't seem like Sun. anymore to me.

Mon. 6. Fair. Went to town by sled with Dad. Overnight at Kate's.

Tues. 7. Fair. At Kate's yet. Fat got pills for me from Brandon, kidney stone coming.

Sun. 12. Fat got some more pills from Brandon for me. To Alex with Bill Gappa Thurs.

Tues. 14. Stormed. Our Gang played for Arma Horst's Wedding Dance $10.00, $2.00 apiece.

Fri. 17. Stormed. Practiced over to Ed's. The folks came & got me with a team.

Sun. 19. Stormed. Kidney stone "in" since Fri. evening. Just can't help but think instead of Violet since I'm home again, have to bawl every time I'm alone upstairs. How I wish I were only where "she" is. If I can only get my debts paid up soon enough. Then I'm leaving here for sure. Art & Vern here in evening.

Mon. 20. 26 below zero. Art, Dad & Frank to the creamery. Wanted them to bring my concertina home, but they didn't cause our gang is playing tonight in town. Stone still in, took a couple hypos then got it out towards evening. Yes! It would be a lot of fun & I'd enjoy playing on dances eventually if My Dear Violet were there dancing to the music to keep me company on stage, but this way, since she's gone it won't ever be fun because it reminds me too much of the good tines Vi & I had together on dances. And every time I see some poor dancer, it reminds me still of "her", Her good dancing, doing the latest steps with Vern.

I'll never forget "her" & know now that as time goes by, I think & grieve more over Vi & it's getting me more than from the beginning. Packed my products & will try retailing tomorrow or day after, with Herb. Packed my clothing too. My only hope & wish to get my debts paid up soon, then get out of this country, at least for a while, & better yet to die a happy death like "she" did, soon, then meet "her" once more. Lord help me, Thy Will be done. Went to Ed's with team then to town with Ed & Dot. Got $2.00 a piece playing last night. Wilbur played, too. Ervin got "tite" Ed drunk, so Melvin took us back to Ed's. Got home around 3 o'clock. Little rest.

Tues. 21. 20 below zero settled Didn't stay in town & go out selling because another stone coming & of the weather, too cold. Frank sick, slept all day. Only 2 tabs left. Removed another stone & two more coming again. Wrote a letter to Violet's Mother & also to Doctor Brinkly this evening. Very little sleep & when I did sleep I dreamt that Vi & I weren't married yet & that they were going to send her home (authorities) & when they wanted to take her I screamed for Ma and when Ma came she said they should take Vi & me too & Ma said to me, "You both go to your (Vi's) folks & if you still want to get married after Vi talks to her folks, then you can, & after you're married then you come work for us." Removed another stone, but here's still one that I can't get out. Screamed loud while I dreamt of Vi, Ma told me.

Wed. 22. 23 below zero again.

Thurs. 23. Stormed 24 below zero. Can't get the stone out, so Dad took me to town, told me to try with Herb's help & if I can't get it, then find a way to go to Alex. & see a doc. Her & I can't do anything, so Fat gave me a 1/2 gr. H. but couldn't do anything even then. Overnight at Alfred's.

Fri. 24. 12 below zero. Got tite.

Sat. 25. Fair. To Alex with Fat. Got the stone out before Haskel got to see me. Two of them I removed. Jake finally got the rod for my car & brought it down after it was fixed. He put it in garage overnight.

Sun. 26. Nice day, 48 above at 3 PM. Another renal stone in since 3:30 this morning unable to remove again. Herb & I up to Ed's with my car, Ann & Cyril came there too, & then we went home with Ed & Dot by sleigh, Visited Mom, ate dinner there, loaded my stock & concertina. All except Leo over at Dots, practiced then he took me up to Fats & then he took my car into Jake's garage again cause the threads are stripped that hold the rear right wheel so there nothing will freeze either. Don't know why (although I've caused enough trouble) but I feel as though I'm not welcome there anymore, about time I pull out for Ann's again. She extra told me to come & even if we do argue come over & keep company and make "Peace" again.

Mon. 27. Snowed a little, nice. Down to Jake's, told me he'd have to get the bolts for the wheel for my car from Alex. Alfred paid my way (5 gal's gas, eats, drinks) & Herb gave me $0.50 to ride down. Got the bolts & Jake's putting them in this evening or early tomorrow morning. Felt tough all day, didn't eat until supper time, no sleep for the last 3 nights either, am so dog tired that I went to sleep while Kate's company was here yet, Jerry, his wife, Bill & wife & Sally. Herb used his 2nd mortgage as down payment to buy the truck back that Alfred lost. In at the Berglund Garage & got $2.00 to help pay for burned out rod in my car not bad. Ed & Dad starting in to buck straight road that Uncle Joe wants put through. Would have retailed today if the car would have been in shape now. A renal stone in since Saturday night.

MARCH 1939

March 1. Cold, fair snowed, just another day without "her", Violet, the on woman that ever did mean anything to me, Yes! The only one that ever will mean as much to me as my Dearest Sweet Violet did. Just can't get her off my mind today again. My only wish to be where " she " is right now. Told Dad to bring some pills along. Even if I did wrong again, it isn't my fault that I do all them things. Lord how listening to the dam radio gets me. Had an argument with Ed this morning How he "raked" down Mom & Dad and I told him where to get off. Supposed to practice over at Dots but went home on account of the reason mentioned sooner in the days notation. Going home Dad started in same "cursed" story over again Lord! How I only wish my 1st wish would only come true before my "Salvation Dad" as I call it. Makes me shed tears every time I go back to the notation she put down for that day Yes, May 1st, the first promise I ever made that I was sincere about, gee, from the bottom of my heart I meant it, & the 1st one I've ever kept. Hope I can live up to it this year too, I'd promise harder than ever, if only she were here again, some one (Vi) (only) that was worth that promise. And if I can't have my first wish, then I only hope that I'll feel that the happy memories of that day, May 1st, will make me feel that that's worth to start life over Start over for my next best loved person left on this world My Dear Old Mom. But I can't help but live in hopes that My Dear Vi prays with me in heaven that I'll get my 1st wish before May 1st & if not then, then at least on or before Oct. 18th. What a happy "death" she had if only I'll be as lucky as she. Was up alone from 9:30 till 2:15 trying to remove the renal stone but didn't have any luck again.

Thur. 2. Fair, thawed today. Sure felt tough this morning, had to vomit too. Took another 1/2 gr. H. 14 tabs left. One slip off & one 1/2 gr. in evening 1 left from 10. Vern & Muriel here in the evening. Ethel & son here from yesterday. Showed Ethel notations made by Violet in her Diary. Asked me to let her take it along & read all of it, but can't let her do that. Violet wouldn't either.

Friday. 3. Fair, cloudy. Took 1/2 gr. hypo, then went to town & over to Kate's. I tried to remove a stone but nothing doing. Got my car from Jake's, put in 5 gals. Gas, ate dinner a Kate's then left for Eling. Harley not home & was told he was in Alex. Went alone, got there, renal stone removed & was given some tabs to use in case swelling would prevent me from passing. Overnight & for supper already at Ann & Cyril's. Seems like to me like this were my real home. Harley here in evening. Decided he could go out retailing with me in forenoon. After he left, Ann, Cyril & I talked over marriage relations problems till 11:30. How nice it would have been if we would have done like Ann thought we should. Vi & I should come live with them during winter & with the folks in summer again. How it makes me wish we would have done that & that we would have been living there with Ann & Cyril, & I think then it never would have happened Too late now.

Sat 4. Fair, thawed. Up at 6:45 this morning. Harley came around 7:30; & at 9:30 we started out retailing. Got as far as Gunther's and there my radiator froze up. Around 10 we had it thawed out & then started from Joe Roers on. Made 8 calls, sold at 7 to the amount of $9.45, $3.68 gross profit. $3.00 net minus 50 cents hired help expense equals $2,50 clear. Sold exactly 2 hours, $1.25 per hr. Had dinner at Ann's and slept in afternoon. Elreen sick in bed Tony Skrovia here helped Cyril haul wood. One of Cyril's pigs gone since yesterday. My left knee getting stiff again.

Sun. 5. Cold, fair, thawed. To church with Ann & Marlene. Cyril looking for his pig. Elreen up today & helped me keep my records straight. Reading Dr. Brinkly's book in P.M. Ed, Dot, Mary, Melvin, Frank, & Ethel & Harley here in evening, played cards & had a swell lunch. Had a swell hot beef sandwich etc. Good night's sleep. Noted a stone.

Mon. 6. Cold, raw, wind, fair. 1/4 hypo. Car froze up couple times. Removed another stone in forenoon. Retailed in afternoon from 3:10 to 4:30 & sold $2.41 clear profit. Harley got .41 cents for his share. Crocked up to the gills this evening.

Mar. 7. Tues. Raw wind. Fair. Over at Karr's, picked up Claud, took him to town, back home again. He ate dinner at his place, then I ate at Cyril's & in the P.M. we started retailing. Got stuck like hell at Redik's & it was 3:05 when we did stock. Took orders for spring delivery for cattle spray to the amount of 5 gallons. In the evening we practiced at John Doll's hall. Harley & Claud drove home with my car & picked up more stock.

Wed. 8. Cold raw wind. Got home 1:30 last nite & around 2:15 I started getting a terrific backache, kidney attack & did my left knee ever pain. Didn't get an hour of sleep & Elreen I think around 4:30 got up & brought me aspirin & water. To the doctor today and had another renal stone removed & also got some pills in case I couldn't pass from swelling (bj). Got home in time for supper. Sure feel tough & both fault sure plenty bother.

Thurs. 9. Fair, beautiful day. First sign of spring, I saw today saw two crows. Had another stone removed today in Alex. Very "dam" little sleep again last night in fact not much sleep since Tuesday. evening. No retailing today yet. After I came home, Ann started laying into me on account of dope again. A couple days ago she told me she didn't care about me using drugs as long as I told the truth about it, & tonight she started lacing it to me because I used it. Pain in the abscess that I'm getting on my left leg is getting worse tonight. Don't think it'll come up to the surface for the next several days though as there's very little to be see yet & there's hardly any inflammation yet. Schwartz & Ben over here in the evening & Ann & I & Schwartz & Cyril played together whist. We won both games.

Fri. 10. 22nd Birthday. Stormed to beat hell in forenoon. Bern & I out retailing. Got stuck six times, hung up every time too, & Bern had to walk up to the closest place to get a shovel. We tried to get home for dinner but couldn't get there. We're only about an 1/8 of a mile off but just couldn't make it. Got dinner first at 3:05. Sold close to $10.00 I think though. Got home around 6:30 too late for supper. Schwartz took Ben home with my car for me.

Sat. 11. Fair. Ben didn't show up this morning. I guess he got enough yesterday bucking snow all day. Repaired & reglued both sides of the concertina last nite with Elreen's help & this morning. The other side with Sis's help. Funny I don't hear from Vi's mother. Must be almost 2 weeks since I wrote to her last. We're playing in Clotho this evening. Sure would like to go to show in the State at Alex. $1,000.00 given away this evening. They are going to draw until they hit a person's name that's registered. Ben & I registered

Wednesday. the eighth. Saw the picture "Four Girls in White" starring Florence Rice. Not a bad picture. Played in Clotho, not a bad crowd. $3.00 apiece $2.00 clear. Yesterday would have been the happy day "she, Violet my dear Sweet Little Wife" was waiting for, She (Vi) used to tell me. Muriel thought Violet would have had the baby.

Sun. 12. Fair, thawed quite a bit. Got home at 3:45 first, from Clotho, & when I did go to bed, I just couldn't sleep on account of the terrible pain I've got in the abscess I'm getting on my left knee. The whole leg is swollen from above the knee to below the calf of the leg. Slept from 6 until 9 o'clock, so I didn't go to church. Ann, Cyril & Marleen went to Devotions but didn't get there because Mal kept Sis & made them stay for supper. While they were gone Lidy & the kids came over & stayed till Ann & Cyril came back, around 5:30. Lidy & I both slept. In the evening Elings, Gunther, Otto Wilkins, Cappie's, Loefflers, Skoveries, Melvins & Genes came. First a lunch & had a 1/4 of beer. Played 500 & then we got a dam good lunch & at 12 I went to bed on account of the unbearable pain from the abscess on my left knee.

Mon. 13. Raw wind. Got up around 8.:30 & at 11 15 I went to Alex. Up to Sather's & got a prescription for 10 tabs & told me to come back after 3 or 4 day's to get it lanced. Ate a .10 cent dinner & at 2 I took in the show featuring Nancy Kelly, Constance Bennet & Alice Faye in "Tailspin". Got home at 5:30. What a mean miserable life I tried to cause the rest to have because of me. Yes even made believe (Muriel's thought kill myself.) Cichy wrote Rita about it & Rita & Vi always read each others letters & when Rita told Vi about me then Vi said, "You know Rita, I'd like to meet the poor kid & I really feel as though I'd like him`" Violet told me this herself before we were married & Rita also told me this. And when the 2 were on there way down here then Vi told Rita, "Rita, you just watch me play up to the Millerville boys. I'll make them fall so hard for me & then drop them even harder than they fell first." Dear Little Vi.

Tues. 14. Snowing like hell again. Pain still the same in knee & for about an hr. my left hand was swollen so had that the ring even hurt so tight it became. Don't know why, but I'm beginning to feel so dam "blue" lately to think its getting to be so close to the "Happiest Days" of our (Vi's & mine) life, "Our Short Romance" last spring. First appearance of each other on Easter Sunday last year. How I only hope it'll be another "Salvation time" as "we" called it, to be able to make & keep the same promise that I made last year on the 4th of May "our engagement day", then save hard, get all debts paid up, & then my last, best & most happiest wish of all wishes; to die a "happy death" like she did real soon if its only Our Lord's Will, which I hope it will be. Ann's 40th Birthday celebrated it last Sunday right (Little Sleep again).

15. Wed. Stormed terribly all day. Harley, Ann, & I to Alex., with my car. Up to Kirland, got a tube of tabs 20 1/4 grs. Roads so tough going over that we put on chains going home. Burned out my generator--$4.15 one to the dogs again--got it for $4.00 & time till the 30th to pay it. To court for my check but they had sent it off already. Made it pretty easy after all going home. We put on chains in Brandon and I didn't get my check in the post office & Hand didn't leave it at Cyril's box either. Ann, Cyril, Elreen & I played cards in evening & after that we discussed the menace of communism entering the country. Went to bed around 12 but don't think I got more than 2 hours of sleep, so terrific the pain was in my knee, even when I took an extra 1/2 gr. hypo. One dam slip off after another today, I at 2 went to the dogs before I cleaned the needle with a hypo wire. Took 8 aspirins besides the shots in the evening.

16. Thurs. Cold & started drifting again. Gosh! But the pain is severe this morning in the abscess in the left knee. God! I hope the check will come today as I'll have to have it today. Ann showed me her varicose veins. I'd get them treated just as soon as possible if I were in her place. Believe it or not, but I don't see how I can go & play tomorrow night if I don't get the abscess lanced or opened today. It'll hurt too much yet if it's opened tomorrow first. Fat & Ed here to see how my lump is & he's going to call up Lorin, tell him to pick me up tomorrow night, if the weather lets up & we play. Got my check today, Hank left it here right away. Sure wish Harley would have come down here & went to Alex to get the abscess opened for tomorrow night.

17. Friday. Storming a little, fair. The "Dutchman" played in Clitherall. Had to go around Evansville to get there & went home around Parker's & Alex. No crowd. Ervin & I got tite, and I fell asleep on the stage. Didn't get a dam cent out of it. Got home first at 3:30. Ate lunch in Alex. At 4:30.

18. Sat. Fair. Left Ann's & went to town. When I got to town I bought a beer, was going to get out my business Billfold & be dam & I had lost it. Lost it last night on the dance $5.50 in it for sure & maybe more. God, what'll I do now. 5.00 borrowed from Dad that he doesn't know anything of. Overnight at Clara's. Poor night's rest again.

19. Sun. Beautiful day. Still over at Clara's. In the evening I attended Mrs. Cappie Pehake's Birthday Party. Got back to Clara's at 2:30. Terrible pain in leg.

20. Mon. Fair. Slept till 11 o'clock, ate dinner, practiced a little in the P.M. then left for Alex. where I had the leg reopened & a small stone removed. Got some pain relieving medicine also. Took some at Bud's Cafe & when I got over to Leo & G.D. place in the evening & was going to take another one for pain from kidney attack I noticed I had lost them. God If I don't have the darndest luck then I don't know. Have a hell of a time getting it & then I've got to lose the dam things. Don't believe I got 1/2 hour of sleep because of the pain from kidney attack & abscess on top.

21. Tues. Beautiful again. Got up around 6:30, ate breakfast at 8, dinner at 10:30 & left Geog around 11. Got up to Sather's office at 11:30 had the stone removed by 12. Dam big stone again & was it ever painful. Don't feel like wanted to live with damnable luck I've got again, besides all this Christly pain that drives a guy nuts besides. Over to Elnor & Gordon's in evening. Sat up & talked till 1:30 about Violet & myself.

22. Wed. Beautiful day. Still over at Elnor's. Got 8 pills from Leibold. Played Clitherall in evening without a crowd again, Overnight at Elnor's in evening again. Slept till Elnor woke me up at dinner time.

23. Thursday. Hot day. Running a temp of 102. To Alex got pills, then to town, got a 1/2 pt & couple of beers then went home. Just one argument after another that's what it'll be as long as I'm home, and that's my biggest reason for wishing my end were here soon, like I told Doc. Kirland. Honestly! I'm so doggone undecided, some times I think I'm going to reform right now, & then again I think I'll wait till my "rope" comes to end & then again think I'm going to try meet ends by not reforming at all if my "rope" doesn't come to an end like "she" used to tell me. Delirious all night from pain & no pills until this morning. One slip off & 1/4 gr. shot tonite. Took Vern home & got stuck so darn bad that I couldn't get out until Pat took a turn to pull me out.

24. Fri. Beautiful day again. Home all day. Took 1 1/2 gr. hypo in morning and 1 slip off.

25. Sat. Hot, cloudy. Home all day again, Vern came in P.M. to help Mom do Sat. work. One 1/2 gr. H. in morning. Broke needle so 1/2 gr. went to the dogs & in P.M. I took another 1/2 gr. H. to remove renal calculi. Wrote to Upland Co. Had a blow out while car stood still, changed tire over noon hour. Ripped tire with a plank while stuck yesterday.

26. Sun. Raw wind To early Mass with Mom & Dad. Mary, Melvin, Ethel, Frank, Art & Vern home for dinner. Had to go practicing rite after dinner. More fun. Froeming didn't come. To town & got a pint snort's. Art & Vern here in evening. Frank & I played with Vern & Mom. 2 games of whist, lost both with 1 skunk.

27. Mon. Cold wind. To Alex in afternoon to have renal calculi removed, took out one & the 2nd one so painful that I had to take anesthetic to remove 2nd one. Down to relief office & was told that this month I wouldn't get any more help (April). Jawed for a 2nd tire & tube, wiper blade, three boots and starter cleaned and shaft bearing repaired. Got home sleepier than hell around 3 feeling so darn weak that I coldn't see sometimes more than five feet ahead of me on account of pain in the genitals.

28. Tuesday. Cool wind. To Urbank with Mom & Dad & hired Eddie Peterson for 7 months @$ 100.00. Over at Vern's in afternoon, there till evening. Ann & Cyril here while I was gone. Think I'm getting a new lump on stiff knee. Very Little sleep last night as pain in ankle.

29. Wed. Cool, warming up. Art & Vern here painting. Uncle Ben here in A.M. for a visit. Frank helped paint in P M,, too. Went to town in P.M., got a couple of "snaps", tried to remove renal calculi but in vain. Doctor removed it for me, quite painful so he sent hypos in case I couldn't piss, or if another calculi should come. Stopped in at Ann's to pick up my liquid stock, then ate supper right away. Got a flat so Cyril & I changed it, then he, Ann & I went over to visit Bella sick in bed with flu & asthma. Called the folks & let them know where I was, Dad and I played cards, Cyril & Rudy pumped up the spare, then went home in bed by 10. Another calculi alright but can't be removed yet, so must wait till morning or until it appears close to the surface. Told Dad where I was & why I went there instead of going to Ethel's like I said I would. Chills & terrible pain in ankle.

30. Thursday. Cool, fair cloudy. Removed the renal calculi this morning. After taking a 1/2 gr. hypo that I got from the doctor yesterday. Art here in forenoon, helped Frank put on second coat of paint in dining room. Wrote to Vi's Mom & also to Doc. Brinkly. I sent in the examination blank for Mom & me, so as to get his big doctor book free. After dinner I drove over to Ethel's. There from right after dinner until about 5:15 then over at Mal's, looked at her chicks & brood of little pigs. Melvin & I talked about caponizing 100 Leghorn cockers. Painted while waiting all of the last. Felt like throwing up first, then started noticing that I was getting weary. No sleep, thinking of Violet all nite.

31. Fri. Cold and windy. Terrible backache this morning, think I'm getting another renal calculi attack, stitch in side. Frank Dens here, cleaned out, then plastered our cistern. Lord help me, how can I ever quit dope if those damable stones keep coming? One there now & there's one coming down from kidney. Was going to remove stone but hypo slipped off so its no use to try because its so dam sore yet from the one I removed yesterday. Art & Vern, Muriel, Ed Dot, Bud, Lucille & the kid here in eve. Played cards & ate a lunch. To bed at 1. No sleep.

APRIL 1939

April 1. Saturday. Bj 1/2 gr. Weather. Cold morning, fair warm, cool evening again. Got up around 9 o'clock. Frank Daas here already when I got up, to plaster the cistern out with glass water (egg preservative). I left for town right after breakfast. "Fronie" over at Bob's with a pretty nice "jag" on when I got there. Shook 3 rounds of dice & I didn't lose any. Ate dinner (hamburger) at Bob's with Alfred was down to his place. Him & I fixed my spare, put in a boot at the beak and then Alfred checked the grease in my transmission. Dam thing almost dry. We put in about 2 lbs. & it holds only 2 1/2 pounds when dry. Then we tried it out by running out to Leaf Valley and doing 55 & over with that terrible gravel & howl in the universal. Al & I out to some janty on account of a trucking job. Took Tina up to the Feist store, didn't get no meat there, went home, told Al that, then he sent us up to Fat, drove around to see if Fronie wasn't at John K's. Not there though. Al & I also took water from Sister cistern (soft) & drinking water from Lewie Brozek. I drove his truck. There for supper, talked about Vi & my marriage relations & compared them with Tina's & Al's. Went home around 7:30 or later. Got plenty for staying in town, my voice, picking my nose, scratching my hinder, my eyes & everything was wrong Hell, hell, hell. Yes! Everything I did, said, look, words, & actions were wrong tonight, yes even my thoughts would have been wrong I'm sure, if they could have read them too yet. Like Frank Thaesh, "Fronie" & Al too said, going out riding, visiting, taking in all enjoyment possible is all I've got on this world, & why shouldn't you do it whenever you can. It's to help me to try to forget the pain, dope & most of all, it's because of Violet. Still I catch plenty hell all the time.

April 2. Snow overnite, cold cloudy. Mom, Dad & I to lst Mass Palm Sunday. Darn little sleep last night again, in fact I read till 3:15, then tried to get any sleep at all. Church reports distributed, Easter Skedules also, & Fat's Grocery Special's for Easter also left in every car during Mass. To second Mass with Art & Vern & got a palm for the folks too. Mom, Vern, Muriel & I to Stations of the Cross. Vern bumped into my Osteo while eating & did it every pain. Mom gave it an alcohol bath but it still hurts awful. 2 sleepers for pain with 3 aspirins. Wrote to Mc. Trying to get back in & to Works. Think there' s a stone coming in.

April 3. Monday. Cool, fair. Bob's came & got Mom at I o'clock. Clara the proud mother of another body. Got up around 8:45. Vern here while Art & Dad to creamery. Peterson called & told us to come get him in P.M. & when Dad came up there in P.M. there he told Dad that he wouldn't work for lst price offered & that he wanted $30.00 per month or $1.00 per day. To Alex. Up to Sather & had another renal calculi removed. Took in "There Goes My Heart" starring Fredric March & Virginia Bruce at the Andria Theater. Got my 3 prints (extra) from Olson & am having 8 prints developed from negatives that Rita gave me of Vi, that those two took while working in Hartland last year in March. Over at Rita's & let her choose one of the 3 prints I got today. Got 2 bust & 2 group, 1 each of the 3 different kinds we had made. Rita chose the Bust where Vi & I are so close together, smiling more than on any other. Sent off the 2 letters I wrote last night. God I wish I could get into this Ward line by working myself into it, & if not that, then back to Mcconnon where Vi wanted me to stay in first place. Got home around 5:35 after leaving Alex at 5:15. Raymond here when I got home. Was planning on going out retailing tomorrow, & now am going for sure while "Butti' is here. Art, Vern, Mary, Raymond & I over to Clara's this evening. There till 8:45, home at 9. Penes pretty sore & inflamed this evening. Raining a little tonite.

April 4. Tuesday. Cloudy, drizzled, rain. Read till 3:30 this morning, Got up at 10:15. Butts hauled wood, straw & manure in forenoon & I got everything stacked up in forenoon. Raymond & I started out retailing at 12:30 or 1. Out in west part of my territory. Got a flat tire just south of Ask Miosner, then went to Brandon, had it fixed but got a blowout north of Brandon going home. Sold for rite around $6.00 in about 2/1/2 hours. Ruined the tire & tube at the last blowout. Not much profit. Will have to pay the kid two bits per day for going with me. Over at Ed's, practicing. I mean I was sposed to come there, but when Ray & I got there, then Bud came out & told us we're supposed to go to town & practice there at John's hall & we did. Rained so hard that it poured. Practiced till 10:30. had a beer then Ray & I went home. Mom told me before I went practicing that she felt like throwing up & when we got home they she started moaning, threw up & told me I was right in predicting another gall bladder attack for her. Told her to remain quiet & then went down, got ready 1/4 gr. hypo & gave her that. Ray & I balanced the budget just like Elreen & I always used to, or like Violet & I used to. Both peetered out so goodnite. Huh? Yep.

April 5 to 8. Wed. to Sat. Weather, cool. Raymond & I didn't come home at all. Stayed overnite in Ashby. Sold enough to make car expense. We came home Saturday. afternoon and went to confession. What are said Easter it will be for me this year. Last Easter I got to see Violet for the lst tine, when she came into church with Rita.

April 9. EASTER SUNDAY. Cool. Al over to Mary's for dinner except Mom, Dad, Ethel & Frank, they were at Bob's. Kid Baptized. Butts & I to town in afternoon, met Bernie Buse. He asked me to take him to Miltona. Irene mad cause she couldn't go along. Got the chills so darn bad stayed overnight at Bemies.

April 10. Monday. Cold. Bernie & I to Alex where Sather removed two stones & gave a script. Bernie overnight here. Played in Millerville at dance.

April 10, 11, 12, 13. Tues, Wed, Thurs. & Fri. Weather halfway decent, snow & fair. Bernie & I out retailing & getting dope again. Played at Clitherall.

April 15. Sat. Yes! A year ago today Rita Cichy brought Violet down to Millerville. We played at Erdahl $2.75 a piece.

April 16. Sunday. Cold, windy. Fronie & I on a tear. Quit playing today. Lord how I wished my end were close, yes, a happy end like my dearest Vi had.

April 17. Monday. Cool again. Dad & I up to Sathers. Both want me to go to the University. Told them a strait No!

April 18. Tuesday. Fair, windy, one quarrel after another.

April 19. Wednesday. Fair. One year ago today I first really got to see my Dearest Violet. She & Rita came to work here. Vi in the forenoon, Delores introduced me to her yet, but she went along with Delores to Alex., & came back in the evening at 7. Rita came with Dad in the afternoon. I laid on my bed, Bernie sat along side & Rita & Violet sat at the table. Vi sat on the opposite side & faced me, & Rita faced Bernie. Vi asked to look at my book of pictures, then she smoked a cigarette & we all went to bed. Up to Art's in afternoon he helped me take out a stone. Came home in evening with Art & Vern because I broke the universal joint on my car. Had in mind to pack my products, & return them today, but I just couldn't do it, to think it's a year ago that I first met "her", & it would have been our means of making a living if only My Dearest Sweet Vi had lived longer.

April 20. Thursday. Cold, windy. Yes! Today Mom, Vern & I packed the products to return. Them, today a year after knowing her for the 2nd day "she" spent here with me. Just couldn't help but bawl till I was half nuts thinking of it all especially after having pain from 2 lumps. I'm getting & to think she's (Vi) not here any more to console & take care of me like she always used to. Yes! Take care of me like no nurse ever could have or did. "Pray for me Dear Violet".

April 21. Fri. Cool, fair. This Friday a year ago was the day I first really starting flirting" with Vi, (as she called it) by Pat playing the concertina & then developing some pictures for her, in the evening. Was supposed to go along to Brandon & send off the products, but felt so dam bad about everything that I started talking one sleeping cap after another until I went under around noon & didn't come to until evening so nothing was sent off anyway.

April 22. Saturday. Hot, sultry. Year ago this evening is the night that her (Violet) and I first really started keeping company with each other while she gave me a manicure which I got for giving her an after shave lotion rub, the night Bernie called me out & told me to lay off. Yes, & Vi & I told him to go to bed like a nice boy should & was he ever mad at me. Mom got clucks from Dot & I took the car, went to Brandon & got pills, after they refused to get some for me.

April 23. Sunday. Fair, cloudy. First time I took Vi out a year ago this Sunday evening, over at Bob's. First hugging & kissing too. Bernie told her that morning before I got up, "Looks like Ray's getting romantic" & she told him, "Not that I know of." Yes. Her & I played a couple game croquet against Bernie & Rita in the afternoon. How terribly hard we both fell in "love" a short while later, yes, then married & parted even more quicker were we. Lord! Who would have thought all this would happen so soon. All home except Lidy, Elnor & Clara. Took pictures of the kids. Clara's twins & Kate's twins on one picture & also each set alone & as soon as I get them developed I'll send Vi's mother one of each because she told me to send her one of Clara's girls if I'd ever take pictures of them. Yes! She said yet that I could imagine how dearly she loved little girls, to think she had to lose the only one Precious Daughter she only had. And how Violet used to tell me she wished our baby to be would be a set of twins, but that she'd like it better with one boy & a girl, because she'd have all she'd ever want & we'd both get help when they'd grow up. Yes, 2 children she wanted regardless what they'd be & when she'd have them, then we'd both agree on our marriage relations (use preventive) like the Priest said we should & could, she always used to tell me.

April 24. Monday. Nice. Oh God! Let me dream of My Dearest Violet every night so beautiful as I did the last two nights. Yes! How she kissed & hugs me. Yes even let me do the "doodooddles" as she used to call it. Up at 4:30 this morning & awake already since 3:30 from pain due to abcess on my left leg. Needled it this morning around 4 for the 4th time & an getting rid of one by doing so, but not this other one the way it looks. Broke the tub of 24 tabs.

April 25. Stormy, cold. Lord, did I ever have pain this morning. Not a wink of sleep last night & thought I'd get some this morning, but not a wink either until I took 2 sleeping caps, then slept till 11. With no pills its almost unbearable. Dad gave me 2 in afternoon. One slip off & the other one alone wasn't enough so I couldn't needle the lump. Listened to the radio for the first time since last November, I think. & did it ever remind of Vi hearing Dipsy Doodle on Pipe Organ Electric.

Poem Written by Ray After Her Death:

Vi & I

Yes, Vi & I we married,
In fact when both were young.
Though none thought our love would stay.
But to both of us it clung.

Our living made by Saleswork.
Many customers did we see
And on each farm there still remains
A lot of Vi & me.

Work was work those early days,
Just the two of us to feed.
So Vi & I we managed,
Folks do when there is need.

Then all of a sudden strangely,
Fate seemed to leave us down,
Vi & I were parted,
Then I was left alone.

Left alone to manage
Come home at night & sigh,

It seems I just don't care to live,
Live without Dear Vi.

Everybody loved her,
They treated us so kind;
But not until we were married;
And now "she's" left me alone behind.

Now I've quit the Saleworks,
It reminded me too much of Vi
Maybe now I can forget,
Some day--By & by.

How can I forget, the day she came,
One April sunny day,
And how blue I felt the lst time she left;
Yes, the 16th day of May.

But she soon came back & we married,
On the 27th of June;
Then how quickly we were parted again
Oct 17th, Yes, so soon.

If only dreams would come true.
I'd leave this world & die;
Leave this work forever,
Yes, to & join Dear VI.

Written April 25th 1939

"Pleasing Mom & Dad"

I've lost my Dearest Violet,
I've given up all I've had
And now I "hope to settle "down",
To please my Mom & Dad.

Please them in my own way,
But they'll never understand;
Lets "HOPE" we meet in Heaven,
But I'm "afraid" I shan't.

April 26. Wednesday. Cold, fair. Pain is unbearable this morning that it just seems I don't know what I'm doing. Never was so shaking in all my life as I was this morning at 10 o'clock after telling Mom that they don't need to get me pills today nor at any other time either but that unless something turns up one near future days. They should get ready for any thing. Lord! Help me, Don't let it happen for Vi's sake. Too shaky to write more but they'll find out. Around noon Dad came in & Mom asked him if he didn't have maybe 2 more tablets. I told them I didn't want them if they thought I didn't need them. Then Mom said it showed I was just too stubborn so I told Dad bring them & I'll open the lump & he did, 2 1/4 gr. And I opened it just before dinner. But I told Mom that what I told her earlier I wouldn't take back & I still mean it. Went to Millerville dance with Frank to listen to "Fat Jolly Dutchmen". Had Eddie Kiger playing too & Leo left out. Swig the slot machine man got me drunk & laid down to sleep on bench with one shoe off; then Mad & Vern took me out & Vern & Art said I should go home with them, but was dam ornery & didn't want to, then Frank came & pushed me with car.

April 27. Thursday. Cool, fair. Asked Mom if she'd go to Alex. with me & get me a tube of pills & when Dad came in I asked him if he'd do me just one favor yet go get me 1 tube of pills & trust me with it. Promised to make them last a week & if I'd need more after that then I'd go to the University Hospital for cure. Mom did help me by telling Dad to give it a try. So Dad & I went & got pills & gave them to me. Took 2 by mouth threw them up both times, then when I got home, I took 1 1/2 gr. Hypo, froze the lump & opened it up a half inch with Vi's Scissor (manicure). Yes, I promised to reform all around, so Lord help me. Lord when I think of what I had planned on doing, yes, that something "furry" & foolish" as Vi used to call it & I honestly had my mind made up to do it & would have done it too because I looked at it this way: sooner one suffer than all the rest. Now they've granted me the one favor, so Lord help me live up to my promise, no lumps or stone so that I won't need to drink & dope any longer. St. Jude Thaddeus, the forgotten Apostle, Relative of our Lord and Helper In Difficult Cases Pray for me so I can forget dope & drink & reform, Yes forget it like you were forgotten. Just hope I can live up to my Promise so I can May 6th (Our "engagement" day. Vi's Birthday, 8th the baby-to-be Birthday. She thought that would be the Day that the Babytobe would be born because that would have been 9 months exactly (Aug. 6th) that would have been was pregnant.) My 2nd Salvation Day or Armistice Day as Vi & called May 31st '38. Yes, that will be another Salvation day. (though not as happy as the first one) for me, Mom & Dad.

April 28. Friday. Fair. Along to town this morning while Mom visited over At Annie's. Talked with Tom Klein about the road, he's going to Alex today to talk with Erickson about it. In afternoon Dad & I took back my products then went to Alex. I was up to Dorothy's but not so hot but he told me May 16th I'd find out for sure. Then Pat & I visited over at Aunt Valeria from 3 to 5. Got a swell lunch, then went home after having to tell her almost everything about My Dearest Violet & myself. Yes Ray! Margeruit always used to come home & tell me what a "goodlooking" wife you had, but then you can't blame her for loving her cause you're a very good looking boy too. Left at 6 for home. Opened a lump on left leg when I got home, with Mom's help with a scissor.

April 29. Saturday. Fair. Slept till 7:30 for a change again, guess it must have been because I had such a beautiful dream about Violet, Yes, the most beautifulest one ever yet. Got up, washed then went to sleep again till 1:15, Got up again and ate dinner and then laid back on the bed . Never had such a rotten night's real sleep, but the dream was worth it if I wouldn't have slept at all.

April 30. Sunday. Nice weather. Didn't go to church on account of the terrific pain & stiffness of my left leg, but had in mind to go anyway until I shaved & washed then got so dam much pain while standing so long. Took my zip-sweater & shirt & put them both on railing of the daybed, before washing. Then pain got so bad that I lay down, fell asleep, woke up when they came home. Vern cleaned up dining room after church, picked up my sweater, hung it up, & when I was going to take a shot around 10, then I found out that my sweater was laying on floor, had dripped while I covered up to sleep. Aunt Tina had stepped on it & the tube of "phines" in the zip pocket crushed all to hell. Nine of them left Saturday night when Mom counted them & none after that. Uncle John came in time for dinner & after dinner I went to town with Aunt Tina & U. J. Dobmeyer. Frank Klimek wanted me to go to Miltona to watch the (Jitterbug) dance prize but didn't go & bawled like a baby from pain & no hypos to take either! Took 6 Sleeping caps & 18 aspirins for sleep & pain & still I didn't get but 1/2 hour but with a nice dream of her first.

May 1939

May 1. Monday. Beautiful day. Yes one year ago today my Dear Violet "ditched" Herb for the 2nd time to show that I was the one she loved. She told me after we became engaged. One year ago today while out riding with Art & Vern, Bernie, Herb, Vi & I, Herb proposed to Vi, & told her not or worry about clothes, because he'd marry when he'd get his estate money & then he'd start worrying about her clothes. She scorned his proposal & even ditched him & went home with me. Supper was already past and we were told to help ourselves. Vi made me & herself each a couple ham sandwiches and brot them to my bed & there her & I ate our supper, then went out for a walk so as to be alone. Yes, May the month of all of our "Love Tragedies". She had to leave me after we told the folks about our love, & plans to marry. Then being "pulled in", our battle at the court house, my terrible quarrel with Mom & Dad. Yes, all this taking place in May. And today after another quarrel with the folks, I went to Doc. Sather and got my last tube of morphine, made out the papers for the University, got them signed, & sent them off. Spent a sort of a "Farewell visit" over at Lidy's. Lidy took me over to Ann's, her & I visited Ms. Tony Skrovia & the folks came & got me in the eve after Erma, Elreen & I had our "Farewell Talk". Needled the abcess on left leg at home. Yes, I feel now as though I don't even belong home anymore. If only it be the Lord's will to let me suffer plenty then let me die soon, suffering so I can meet my Dearest Vi soon, in "Heaven". I'm sure.

May 2. Tuesday. Hot, cloudy, rain. Lord, did I ever have pain this morning. Mom & I over at Ann's & then to the Dr. in Fergus. She got another shot in the leg & is in real tough shape I think. Eddie Wilfert playing in Urbank this evening. Frank went & came home at 1:30, I was still sleepless then yet & Mom too. She coughing all night.

May 3. Wednesday. Fair, rained overnite a little. Most painful morning I've had since Aug 16 '38 when my Dear Violet felt so because of me sleeping in the barn on account of fear from "old Man" if I should moan in my sleep from pain without pills which he wouldn't allow Vern, Vi & Ma to get for me. Got up at 4:30 that morning, walking around groaning & that's how I felt this morning too. Was going to take a shot quick for pain & to remove a stone that came down last night so I'd be in shape half ways to go along to Alex. Help argue road business & visit & take a wedding picture to Aunt Valeria. Sort of make that my Farewell visit. Set the open bottle of phines on the reservoir, took out the syringe, put in the tube, was going to reach the syringe rite in the reservoir, just during that time the "Old Man" asked me a question. I turned & looked at him while I reached to fill the syringe & accidentally knocked the bottle with the entire number of tabs into the reservoir. Couldn't find the "dam" things rightaway, & before I did find them they were all dissolved & when I tasted it, there was no taste of any kind left. For my luck that Mom counted them just before & that both saw how accidentally happened. Up to Sather's, but he wasn't home, (to Fergus Medical Mart) so I went up to Kirland's, called Mom, was to get Dad's permit. Dad went up, got the script, got it filled, while I went & bot a BondBox at 75 cents. He gave me 2 tabs, over at Comer PoolRoom, took a shot there, 1/2 slipped off, over at Aunt

Valeria's gave Katie the picture to Brandon to pay freight bill which hasn't come in yet so couldn't pay. Then went home, took my key case, put in the key to my strongbox, called out Art & asked him to help my try to remove my renal calculus, walked out behind Congress Bld., & there removed the calculus. Came into the house & the "Old Man" asks me if I removed tube of pills from his jacket. Thank God! If Art, Vern, & Mom want to think & remember a little & be truthful, they have to admit I laid on bed until Art & I went out to & positively had no chance to take them. He must have lost them in Alex because he wasn't out of the car from Alex till home we looked high & low around here & nothing to be found. I honestly think, he's just bluffing trying to make me believe they're lost so he wouldn't have to give me them & he keep them himself. He's trying to tell me I've got & took them. Took 3 S.C. and four aspirin for pain. Got a letter from Mother In Law. Lord, what'll I do tonight if he really did lose the tubes of pills. Opening the abscess on side of left leg. First froze it good & hard, had Dad sharpen Vi's little scissors, put in another cubic cent of Novocain & then cut open the abcess about an inch in width, & about 1/3 inch in depth. Without any pain, whatsoever, & it just goes to show that doctors would only take time & plenty Novocain, they could open abcesses without pain. Slept from 4:30 to 7 this morning.

May 4. Thursday. Fair. Slept till 7, only 2 1/2 hr. of actul sleep. Frank came home 12:45. Found the one tab I lost from 2nd batch of pills. Laid on chair under old pill box. Took that hypo this morning.

May 5. Friday. Hot. Slept all forenoon. Awake from 1:30 to 4 then slept again till 8:30 in evening due to sleep tabs.

May 6. Saturday. Cloudy, yes, cloudy like it was a year ago today on Violet's 18th birthday, and today the Baby-to-be would have been if "she'd" of had her wish. Now, me left alone to argue, yes almost steady, with Mom & Dad. And today I found the crushed bottle with the bitter tasting pills all crushed except 1 & that slipped off when I was going to take it. And they believe me? Yes, Sooner the dog outside, he'd believe he told me. Pain, like I haven't had since My Dearest Violet left me. God! When I think of last year. Vi & I had planned the doings of the whole day the day before. How we drove along with Art & Vern to town, then asked me to buy a pint. Because what was what I always used to think was needed to have a good time before I went with her, & today (year ago) she said I should have one. In fact she said we should set up to think it "Our Engagment" Day" as we called it, plus her birthday, & now would have been another born. In fact what she always used to pray for. Yes, In the evening Esther, Frank, Mary, Melvin & Herb & Bernie came up & she bot a pony too yet. I helped her pay for everything cause I thought it wasn't more then right as she said then already, "Ray just make believe you & I are one. Yes even "Man & Wife" because we will be pretty soon married anyway." Yes, & only a little more than a month we were married too & she was right about it. Oh! God, did I ever do a lot of quarreling today. From early morning with Mom until evening at 8:30 with Dad. Yes, I thought the end of my "Blazing Trail" had or would at last come to an End today, & I know, that to make permanent peace in the house, the end of my Trail Blazing will have to have the same kind of end, yes a permanent end to permanent peace, is the only solution to this problem. Told Dad to either get me pills to stop pain or let me use the car to get the shells to stop life permanently. While milking he told Mom I & her could go & after getting supper for Dad & Frank, ready, Mom & I left for Brandon. Had to Mechstroth, & he claims there to pay yet that Fat took. B.S. I think. Jewed the druggist to 60 cents for 20 tablets for hypo.

May 7. Sunday. Little rain overnite, cloudy this morning. Fair now tho took a 3/4 gr. hypo, but got only about 3/8 gr. from it. Couldn't go to Mass on account of the stiffness from the abscess on my right hip when sitting on it. Was going anyway, but Mom told me I shouldn't go. Year ago the 7th Vi & I sat up & planned & planned still more on how we could get married real soon and she'd say, "Yes, & a year ago like this Sun. we took in the show "In Old Chicago" with Maly & Melvin & he said we didn't need to think he'd ever take us along. Cause I didn't buy tickets, or buy beer & lunch, nor buy gas, & I told him right away I couldn't cause I was broke & Bernie would have to pay our way, (he owed me about $4.00) as I didn't even have cash to pay our own way, & I told Melvin before we rode along that I couldn't chip in on anything & that I was broke. Violet & I tried to figure out how we could get married, but, like she wrote in this diary yet, it's a hard thing to figure out, so it seemed like that time, but we won out & figured it out later on anyway. Mom took my concertina home from Fat. All invited out to Ethel's for dinner. Read a Double Mass for my Dear Violet at home. Elnor & the kids came around 10.30, She had a pint of year-old St. Whiskey & they were really all feeling good. I told her to save mine & she saved 1/8 pt. Over to Ethel's for dinner & lunch. Swell dinner, there till 4:30 then went home & tried to remove kidney stone from 4:30 till 6, then had to give on account of soreness. Was going to try with Art's help, but they didn't come. Mom sponging with alcohol, my foot. then Frank Daas finally came. Yes, was just imagining my Dearest Vi sitting, legs crossed, picking off scabs, dead bones, alcohol. Sponging it, dipping out the core of bunion on big toe she'd rub & rub as long as I'd say it still felt good, she'd keep on.

May 8. Monday. Fair. Almost broke my neck bright & early this morning. While going down the stairs my right crutch hit molding and with only 1 shoe on to balance myself & was carrying my bandbox at the side, otherwise I maybe could have hung on to the crutch, but down I went, & so quick that all I remember is seeing the box & crutches go down first & I hit head so dam hard against something that I was really stunned for several seconds or a minute but went all the way down until the last 4 or 5 steps. Mom just came into house, heard the box & crutches when they banged down and cane running right away & picked up the crutches, bandbox, then helped me get up. Was really so stunned from the beginning that I had no pain whatsoever, not even lumps did I feel, but 1/4 to 1/2 hr. later I began to feel it. Mom brot water, tied off the vein, was going to take a couple pills out of bandbox, unlocked it & the "dam" bottle of freezing liquid had broke & soaked up the whole "dam" box of 14 tabs. And the worst of it, I have to get the stone removed in Alex. Anyway & could get pills without cost from Sather, but the Old Man will believe this all as much as the dog, like he always tells me, even when the proof--water on stairway--which proves I didn't brake bottle on purpose & couldn't have done it all up last nite 'cause I locked the box rite in front of Ma after she counted them & the keys to unlock it were at the smokestand, neither could I have done it after, cause the liquid was on stairs & Mom & Vern were both rite there when I unlocked it & Vern saw what was left of the pill, not even 1 whole one to be truthful. Still, have the Old Man believe it? No! Not anymore than the dog he tells me. Went to Sather, removed 2 stones, 1 the biggest one he ever took out yet, painful, never so painful before. Asked me if I needed more pills? Gave some without even asking for them, no, Old Man won't believe that anymore than the rest of breaking Novocain and pills dissolving cause he wasn't along & word holds not water. Also gave 1/2 ounce of novocane. Sather never treated me nicer than he did today & told me he had no answer from University but that I could expect to get in tomorrow or any one of the near future days. Got Art a new part book for his tractor that I lost. Mom & I to Urbank to listen to Whoopee John, then went home. Joe Gappa gave me .50 c to buy a ticket. Lordy, did I ever have pain, think for sure I'm getting an attack or either I hurt my back more then I thot, but felt like an attack coming up all last nite already. Yes a year ago, Vi & I were to a show with Mary Melvin. They got mad cause I didn't chip in & I told them I was broke. But in evening Vi & I alone & this was another nite I tempted "her" like the devil. But she wouldn't give in and would ask why I wanted her to commit if she couldn't live up to it anyway after we've married, she'd say.

May 9. Tuesday. Cool wind, cloudy. Woke up at 8:15 with such a backache either from the fall yesterday, or I'm getting an attack again. Sent off the letter to Vi's Mother, telling her about me quitting everything & about being sick so much & about going to the University. Laid down to sleep in afternoon & was just dozing off; then Mom called & said I had company. Kate & the kids here, & after a while Art, Vern & the kid came to get silage, then Vern stayed till Kate left, at 4:55. Then I figured how much damaged goods there was, made a list of it, wrote them a letter sending the list along, asking to return the items listed, cause I figure they should be worth more then just the freight to get them back, amounts to $3.33 net or $7.45 gross. No notice from the University yet. Gosh did Mom ever hurt my stiff leg by moving the bench on it & then kicked it accidently on top yet when I screamed & jerked the leg back. Am almost real sure that I'm getting an attack because I've been throwing up this P.M. & yesterday already, couldn't eat any supper, noticed first this evening that my back is swollen around the region of my kidney, and also notice pus in urine this evening, with the start of fever, then chills, vomiting, now pain in side also. Up with Mom till 8:30 watching her iron.

May 10. Wed. Cold, raw wind, cloudy. Would of froze last nite if the 300 length stretched wind would of only laid up or quit, but it was really a storm all nite long. Up at 5:45. No breakfast nor anything to eat since yesterday morning. Because I can't keep it down. To town with Mom & Dad to Brandon to get the chicks from Renke's where they took 144 eggs to hatch. Got 11 out of that many eggs, not bad at all I think & not a single cripple in the whole bunch. And Dad stopped in to pay my freight bill too, then stopped at Cyril's to castrate over 20 pigs. Ann went to the Dr. all alone. No letter for me from the University yet. Invitations to attend Leo Kappahm's ordinations & First Mass Service. Had the chills terribly all day long, & in evening when I went to bed yet. Frank went to Millerville dance & show put up by the Genuine German Concertina Outfit that played in Urbank 1 1/2 yrs. Ago. Came home at 4 o'clock.

May 11. Thurs. Heavy frost last nite. No wonder I almost froze to death, with everything white this morning from the frost last nite. Dad called Frank at least 50 times & had to shake him before getting him awake, but didn't get up, then Mom called too but couldn't get an answer out of him & at 5:45. I called him getting no answer too, but still didn't get up. After milking Dad got him out of bed giving him hell, but he took it jokingly yet as he still was still plenty tite yet. Told Dad he wanted A.M. off to go collect from Drummish as the note was due & wouldn't be any good if not collected now. Dad said he'd have to be back in P. M, & he said he would. He said he'd take me to Alex to Dr. but went lst to Millerville & Urbank to drink, then I drove the car to Alex. Stopping at Garfield to drink some more & after having a stone & a pint of pus removed I couldn't find him anywhere's, so I notified Chief of police, Elan Hanson. After going thru all beer joints twice & going back to car was, there he stood swaying like drunk. Pumped up tire, drove up to station, put in gas & air, then drove to

Millerville, had a flat, changed it, then drove to Millerville again. One beer, then home, slept till 6, got up & drove off again & came back at 11 in the evening. Vern & Lid here in evening till 9. Still no papers from University. Terrible pain from abcess yet.

May 12. Friday. Mom & Dad along to town with Art & Vern, then got potatoes from Un. Aug. Martin Kroll in the coop. Arrested for stealing chickens, had 12 penned up at the old Koskie buildings. Roman Roers waited until he came to feed them, but when Roman showed himself Martin denied that they were his, but Ben Urness picked him up & gave him the coop as a night's lodging. Terrible pain yet in my abcess.

May 13. Saturday. Fair. Very little sleep again, or rather no sleep at all until morning then I slept till 8:05. Slept in forenoon till 12, ate dinner, helped do the dishes, helped clean a rooster & then asked if I could have the car to go over to Ann's. Yes, really felt good to think he trusted me that much again & also went up to Lidy's, post office first to see if there will be no letter for Mom from U. While at postoffice Jack talked me for the $1.20 I still owe him, was going to borrow it from Lidy but she had to call up home first, told her not to bother. Went back & told him he should wait until I get back from U. when I'll sell my car. All right he said. Visited over at Lidy's a while, then over at Ann's. Had flat tire but Cyril put on spare, but had to pump it up. Between Pichke's & Roers I had to pump it up again, then check the valve, it leaked & at Jaky's I put in plenty of air to go home on. Boy did I catch hell when I came home & told him about the flat tire. Said he couldn't go to church & cussed several times. Told that I was to Lidy's. There he claimed I was farther too & that he'd ask Lidy & Ann when they'd come tomorrow. I said he should too.

May 14. Sunday. Fair. All to church except Frank. He stayed home & fixed the tire on his car, could of went to 2nd Mass but didn't go. All girls home except Clara, & Ed wasn't either. Cyril & Ann squealed on me about getting 40 pills in Brandon. Cyril was at the Drug Store to get medicine for the kid (Roger) & Zabel must of told him about it I think. Believe it or not, I'll do that guy plenty of dirt when I get back from the University. Melvin took my grease gun for his tractor. In evening Art took my battery for his fence, then Mom & I went to Melvin's with Art & Vern. Ice cream for lunch, home at 10:35 & Frank wasn't home then yet. I didn't get a wink of sleep until close to morning on account of pain in left arm & also pain in back again due to inflamed kidney. Am passing pus in my urine since yesterday.

May 15. Mon. Fair, cloudy. Mom, Dad, Art Vern & Muriel to church. Rogation days have started. Told Dad I'd fix the tire I punctured Sat. when I had the car in P.M. but he wanted to do it in A.M. because the spare on the car was going flat, but he came in & told me he couldn't get the tire off & that he'd bet I couldn't either. Told him to wait in P.M. when I'd open my arm and show him I can change a tire but he insisted I come out & show him how its done. Told him there was nothing to show but that I'd change it for even if my arm wasn't open, stiff & plenty painful yet. Don't think it took me 10 minutes to change the tire & patch it too yet. Art here, fixed the windcharger. Vern over to Loeffler's but her truck not there like Heli stated. Mary & Ethel here today during dinner tine. Opened lump about 1/2 cup of pus too.

May 16. Tuesday. Fair. Mom. Dad & I to Rogation Mass and still no sign of rain which is what we're praying when going to Mass for. Straightened out Dad's Books for (School Bks) as far as I could. Got a letter from University

Hospital to come down any day except Sat. or Sun. Dad & I to Alex. To Sather's. removed a stone, gave a script, & drew map with explanation's of where & when to go down & what to do about the .75 cents 1st day & two bits thereafter registration fee, for every day I come back for examinations of observation while there, also about them stating they wouldn't guarantee hospitalization charges. Vern & Mom washed off my jalopy while Art was to mill & I to Alex. Mom & I over at Melvin's in evening & asked if he would drive to cities. Said he would & could Thurs. & decided on 3 or 3:30. Back 8:30 to bed at 9.

May 17. Wed. Cloudy, All to church except Art & Frank. I had in mind to go to confession & receive but drank water during midnite. Stayed for Mass, & during Benediction I drove to Brandon & got pills there for the last time I hope (40) from Zabel, through Mechstroch crooked work again like usual. Well, the way it looks this morning, Mom, Melvin, I & maybe Vern if her Old Man won't object. Pa said he wanted to go along but didn't to show up, then Mom said he could just as well stay home with Frannie because he couldn't be left home alone, so when Mom said that, then he got mad & said, "Alright, if you want to go so bad then go. If you say I have to stay home, then I'll stay already." Mom told him she didn't say he'd have to stay home & that he was the one that said that himself. So we'll wait & see & until tomorrow morning at 3 o'clock we call it "that". Took out my cabinets & put the seat cushions in my car. Mary here & Dad gave her $3.00 for gas & oil. Vern also here to let us know that she's going along too. My order of damaged goods at depot. Called Lidy & told her to take & pay for it until they stop in coming home from the cities. Told me to make a tour quick & call it a Farewell Tour before I leave. Yes, everybody could go along & that all doesn't interest me one bit. If only my Dearest Sweet Violet were only here yet to go along with me, how much different it would be. It would seem like our "Honeymoon" & would be a happy trip instead of a disgusting and sad trip it will be now for me. No. I don't care one bit whether I get back or not. It would be a happy trip for me after all if I knew for sure that I wouldn't have long to live there & if I could come home a corpse after dying a happy death like she did, yes. Meet her soon, then it would be a happy trip.

May 18. Thurs. Hot, cloudy. Went to sleep at 3 & 3:30 Vern cane in & woke me. Left at 4:30 for the cities. Mom, Vern, Mary, Melvin & I with Dickie & Muriel. Got over to Ely's place 7:30. Vern, Mary & the kids stayed there & Mong Ely, Melvin & I got up to the Hospital at 8:15. Registered, Dr. Wetherby & 3 other students took a history of my case & examined me, put me through the Fluroscope, took 2 urine specimens, 4 blood tests & then made out appointments for tomorrow, 1 for xrays & one for Surgical Staff. The 3 of us went out to eat dinner, came back, got my rooming house appointed--Mrs. Clark. Mrs. Clark took me & Mom up to my room, Melvin & Ely followed. Mom gave me $5.00 then they left for home. Slept out on porch till 4:30, & did I ever have pain all nite.

May 19. Fri. Hot, sultry. Lord did I ever have the chills after washing up this morning. At 8:30 I was taken up to the hospital. Mrs. Clark got a wheelchair, had me register, took me up to xray office, told me that was all I had for today. Fainted while waiting to see if xrays were OK. Took about an our hr. to came to. At 1 Ms. Clark got me home, didn't eat no dinner, had a cot put out on porch for me & can sleep outside from now on. Went up, laid down & rested from noon until supper. Ate supper, then went up & wrote a letter home.

May 20. Sat. Hot, sultry. Up to hospital for surgery. The students opened one lump after begging since Thursday afternoon. On a spree in the evening, Earl Jenson, Aug. & Hank came.

May 21. Sun. Hot. Slept a little in forenoon. Earl & I both homesick. Lord did I ever have pain in lumps. Ely Naddo didn't come like he promised. Pain getting worse in P.M. & in the evening I was half nuts from pain. Not a wink of sleep all nite. Kept everybody awake groaning.

May 22. Mon. Hot, Mrs. Clark took me up to the hospital to get something for pain. Went uptown to see "flatfoot", & he gave me "20 drinks. Got back to Clark's at 6:30, Slept on porch.

May 23. Tues. Cool. Took G. U. & sent me to Rand Rest Room, met Petersen. So stiff that I was in wheelchair all day. Wrote a letter for money from home that I'm sending tomorrow. Not a half hour of sleep all night.

May 24. Wed. Rained, T. & L., cloudy. No breakfast, blood test, neurology & this afternoon xray at 3:30. At 5 Ward came & got me, told me he forgot to got bread & asked if I'd care if he'd get it before talking me home. Was O.K. with me & on 2nd St. 6th Ave S.E. a dump truck loaded with dirt going down 6th Av. S.E. failed to look around while hitting it around 30 m.p.h. I judged & stepping on it going slightly uphill, didn't even slow down & failed to stop, & Ward having slowed down to 10 mph slammed on the brakes but the other fellow didn't slack down nor turn out like Ward did so it was impossible for Ward to avoid hitting him. God, have I ever hurt my abcesses in the accident from the jar of the sudden stop when we hit. Took my last 1/2 gr. hypo when I got home & still haven't got much relief yet. Took 2 aspirins too. The toughest nite I've had since here. Took about 20 aspirins.

May 25. Thurs. Fair. Up for Surgery. Ward had to carry me up to the car. Opened 4 lumps for me. Got all kinds of dressing and also a prescription for 10 M.S. tablets. Got home around 1:30, couldn't eat. Boy did the folks ever send me a nice suitcase & a new set of clothing, cute, too. Had a letter from home & one from Elnor too. Earl here at 3. Even candy from Mom. Fair nite's rest. Took 3 1/4 gr. shts.

May 26. Fri. Rained last nite. This morning I was going to take 1/4 shot & then first noticed that there were 2 left. Some dam dog stole them from me during the nite, and am sure the man I suspect is the guilty one, too. Up to Neurology, got 6 from Dr. Hutchinson. When evening came I was going to take a shot, then I noticed that they weren't the right ones. Took 4 of them but got no relief. Ward gave me a 1/3 gr. shot, but very little sleep.

May 27. Sat. Rained all day. Up to Social Services & they found out I got the wrong ones. She sent me to surgery & I laid on the table from 9:30 to 1:30 & when I asked for a prescription then they said I should have got it at surgery, I was down in 212. Im. Ward. Finally they gave me a shot & Ward & I went home. Pain enough to croak but got a little relief when I drank 3 steins beer. Don't know what I'll do tonite. Still no money from folks. Cloudy. I know that much, if I have to suffer like I did today again I'm not staying very long. Even Ward was madder than hell at them. Can't see why the folks can't send any money either, here I promise to pay Earl back today & now its shit.

May 28. Sun. Fair. No sleep all nite from pain due to abcess that closed up. Ward took me up to IM. Ward & they reopened it & gave me 1/6 gr. M.E., Ely & Earl here for about an hour in afternoon. Took my last sodium amytyle for pain & sleep. Up to Surgery & N.M. & got 6M S. from Hutchinson. Yes! One year ago!

May 29. Sun. my "Love, Dearest Vi", & I went up to Douglas Hotel & stayed there & now to think I'm left alone already, not even 4 months of married life together & how happy both were this day.

May 30. Tue. Fair. Went to church but got there when it was out. Got a ride home. Yes, the day Vi & I had all by ourselves before being married, planning what to do. Pete & I read a while, then played a game of checkers & 3 games of pig. First day I could walk alone since the 24th. Read a Mass for Vi again, also Mass of today. Lord how I wish I could me "her", yes soon, leave this world forever so Mom & the rest wouldn't have to suffer with me like they say they're doing. No, anything but live. How my Sweet VI & I both woke up a year ago today, Band playing to beat heck.

May 31. Wed. Hot, sultry. Up to N. & M got M.S. Pain in hip increasing. Had my Concertina brought up by Rosenthal & $1.00. Also a letter from home & Elreen today. Pete & I up till 1:30 this evening. Yes, today was Vi & my Armistice Day as we called it. The day the folks gave their consent to our marriage. Vi & I were taken home by the folks, Ed & Kate with the promise to see us married & give us $500.00 to start out in life for ourselves.

June 1939

June 1. Thurs. Fair. Up to G. U Clinic. Monday. I'm entering the Hospital. Ate dinner, visited with Harold Closter, and around 2:30 I went up town. Just came out of the "JailHouse & Inn", put change in billfold when somebody grabbed from behind. Was just ready to swing my crutches & when I turned back here was Dr. Sather of Alex. Stood behind me. Him & I talked about the University & he thought I looked better than he ever saw me. I lost 11 lbs. While at Mrs. Clark's but gained 13 lbs while over at Ward's place. But with the abcess on my hip advancing like it is, my appetite leaving, I'll lose them 2 lbs that I've gained since I'm in Minneapolis pretty quick & a good many more lbs. after I get to the Hospital. Got home just in time to have supper (skipped) as I got nauseated. Very little sleep from pain at ankle.

June 2. Fri. Hot, rain. Awake at 3 A.M., restless nite from pain & can't get my urine started at all this morning & should have made an appointment for G. U. but just got 2 rolls of bandage, 6 oz. rubbing alcohol & a set of new crutch tips. Was also going to get a new needle, but they don't stock them & told me to get one at any drug store. Paid back $1.00 to Earl Jensen yesterday, only .15 left for cig. Finished up Erma's & Ruth's letter included Lidy in it as I got a letter from her yesterday & 1 from Mrs.

Prestegard too, & sent it off this morning. Visited Roy Munson & Mc Nellie at Un. Station 21 room 212 after my things at Surgery & Dispensery desk, Roy Munson claims that Pete Prestegard is a 4th cousin. He's going to find out for sure. Lives in Austin. Roy visits me in P.M. Pete & I fixed my concertina & then he went home to get crutches.

June 3. Sat. Fair. Am running a temp. of 105, pulse 142, Breath 48.

June 4. Sun. Hot. Up to Clark's. To confession last night & communion & Mass this morning. Got S.M. Without allowance.

June 5. Mon. Up to surgery & xray & N. & M.

June 6. Tues. Cool. Up to Surgery. Had an abcess opened by taking gas. Walked home from Hospital Got 8 M. S.

June 7. Wed. Hot. Uptown will get into trouble yet if I don't lay low pretty soon. Earl & Shorty here in evening. Peterson went home today. I owe him $3.00 & still have no money to buy cig or tobacco. Plenty pain last night.

June 8. Thurs. Rained again. Up to Surgery, got some alcohol, dressing & 9 M.S. but the wrong one again.

June 9. Fri. Fair, couldn't find my records up at N. M. until just before noon. Told Hutch. About getting the M. S. & he gave me 8 tabs personally from his own. Ward stabbed the vein for me. Must answer Elnor's & Lidy's letters today or tomorrow some time. Sent off their letters this evening.

June 10. Sat. Cloudy. Then rained all day. Awake at 4:o'clock, was cloudy then, quite a bit of pain in the 3 lumps I've had coming up for the last several days & notice one new lump again, Didn't have to go to the clinic for the first time since I'm down here, sold my sample case to Olie Helgeson for $1.00, sent the buck to Pete. Still owe him $2.00, up town way my "flatfoot", got 20 "drinks (shots) from him. Was going to take a hypo in PM, so I could lance the abcess on my left arm, & then I first saw that the tablets were the wrong ones again, oral instead of hypo, & the needle is the wrong one, too & will have to get it exchanged either today or tomorrow if I can only borrow .75 from somebody to pay for the rite ones. Dissolved the ones I had left from the last time & then froze & opened the abcess with Violet's manicuring scissors. Wrote a scenery postcard to Mary & Melvin & a letter to Art & Vern. Yes, one short & long sad year ago today the priest told Vi & I not to listen to the rest of the family & not Mom either cause she had already given her consent to our marriage, when we were to Instructions. What happy days, contented days they were for us both, & now how unhappy, dreary miserable, & uncontented my lonely days are a year later to be spent alone, without my dear sweet Violet here. If only my end were here soon & I'd be only able to die a beautiful happy death like "she" (Vi) did & had then theses days would be happy for me after all. Lord! Thy Will be done, St. Jude help me get only 20 more of what I've already received today. Mom, I'm entering the Un. Hosp. to get myself fixed up of the fun habit & then I'm going home for the summer, spend that at home & come back for the winter to get my leg amputated, & have the Pyemia & Osteo stopped if possible. Just hope they can fix up the fun habit so as to be home for June 27th. Vi & My Wedding Day lst anniversary it would have been. Inez dressed my R. ankle & changed the stocking on it too.

June 11. Sun. Fair, I mean a dreary, drizzling day, cold & even snowed. To the 10 o'clock Mass. Gosh did Syurud Kelly, Bert Riddle & I ever have fun kidding another fellow this evening, also a girl. Lord did I ever get pain towards evening from the 4 lumps & towards morning (at 3:30) I froze them & opened 2 of them.

June 12. Mon. Fair. Up to Surgery. Postponed the Hosp. Admittance till Thurs. Up to Hosp from 8 till 5, nothing to eat till supper, Up to Kelly's room kidding that young girl again. Boy was I happy when I came home & opened a letter I got from home with $4.00 in it, letter from Mom, Vern & Butts.

June 13. Tues. Cool, fair. Will be admitted Thurs. & won't have to go up till then if nothing comes up. Answering Mom's letter & sent it off too riteaway. Up to 4th St. 13 Ave in forenoon. Lena down at my bed all afternoon of today. Sure is nice in conversation & really enjoyed her little visit. She's just the same type as dear Vi, frank, forward & straight.

June 14. Wed. Cool, rain. Up to 4th St. 13th Ave. in forenoon. I visited "flatfoot" & he gave me 40 "drinks" again. Best "load" I've had since I'm down here. Felt good all day too. Letter from Sis, Elnor. Borrowed .20 cents to Roy last nite. Paying back Fri. or Sat. he said, at the Hosp. Met Leora coming home from uptown, said she'd pay me a visit in P.M. & Leora Mrs. Goth, & Mrs. Olson visited with from 12:30 to 4. Wrote a letter to Mother-In-law today, & will have to finish & sent it off tomorrow for sure. Yes, my last day out here at Ward's Rest Home. Am being admitted tomorrow University Hospital for good to scrape my right ankle, tibia & tarsus, & how long I must stay there they didn't know about. Leora & I together all forenoon & afternoon & again in the evening till 9:30.

June 15. Thurs. Fair. Leora & I together from 8 A.M. to 4:15 P. M. She was the first one to visit me in the Hospital.

June 16. Fri. Cloudy, hot. Leora here from 2:45 till 4:15. Went uptown for me. Got me 10 "drinks". Wrote a letter home.

June 17. Sat. Cloudy. Nurse questioned me as to if I take medicine. Told her the truth. Was up early on account of pain in lumps & osteo. Leora got me 10 "drinks" this P.M.

June 18. Sun. Cloudy. Up in A.M. to wash, but couldn't get up anymore in P.M. Relly & RIddell here. 5 drinks left from L., took them, pain.

June 19. Mon. Fair. In bed all day, are trying to cut me from M.S. entirely, but shit on that noise. Leora here again brot me 5 "drinks" again, more pain. Wrote Vern, needled lumps Sat. afternoon.

June 20. Tues. Fair. Up 4 first time since Sun. Saw Leora, xray, getting me 15 "drinks" & she did to 3 o'clock. Asked her if she was serious about what she wrote in letter I got today? She said yes, told her not to let herself go that far & ruin her own life for doing so. Said she had never met another fellow that meant to her what I mean to her.

June 21. Wed. Rained all day. Slept till Leora came. Bubbins came up to see me. Was I surprised. Leora brot me a pack of Avalons & 15 "drinks" again. Letter from Mom & Lidy. Herb working there again at $35.00 per month. Sure felt insulted cause Paine questioned me & also stated that I was sposed to have used vulgar language in front of the nurse which ain't so unless in my sleep & I told him so too. Get my 1st. fever treatment tomorrow sometime, so they transferred me to that floor where they are administered (4th). Was told & I have a room all by myself, close by 6 windows with the nicest view & visibility possible to have.

June 22. Thurs. Gloomy. Lovejoy & Doc Paine up to see me & found the "Script." Arrested, Yes I was put thru the same experience as Dear Vi was before we could marry, that day.

June 23. Fri. Sunny. Appeared before Commissoner Abbot, $7,000 bail set 4 me. Slammed in the hoosgow at 11 AM.

July 1939

July 15. Fair Weather. Indited by the Grand Jury.

July 19. Wed. Fair weather. Got a ticket to appear before Judge Wosby (tough egg he is) Pleaded Guilty & pain. The fine for intoxicated while driving (Sent 2 U.S.P.H.S. Hospital at Lexington Kentucky, but not before fall if I can make it.)

July 22. Convicted by (Grand Jury.)

July 26. Left for Lexington Kentucky on the Steam Liner.

July 27. Arrived at 11:30 AM 2 day. Stayed there until the 31st of May, 1940 & believe me I don't believe I suffered more physically & mentally during that time than during my entire period of illness. Not that I didn't have the best of care & room & board. Was put on a special high calorie diet but who could eat when they feed us one medicine after another. Trying 2 find a cure 4 me. After 5 months they talked about sending me to Leipzig, Germany but with the war with England refused. Took 2 or 3 shows a week, one good symphony or Band Concert & one burlesque & vaudeville besides Best Friend Jack Hinten & I sure would go on some tare's. Got so unbelievable tite & higher then a kite until we'd pass out colder then a cucumber.

MAY 1940

May 31. Friday. Was accompaint home by M. Crossline Medical Technician, a passenger on some streamline from Lexington Ky. to Chicago Ill. From there on the Burlington Zepher which took me as far as St. Paul Minnesota. From there the folks met me & took me home. Had the time of my life on the way home. No more South for me. I'd sooner endure the cold during the winter then the hot summer down South.

June 1940

June 1. Sat. Hot day. Arrived home with Mom Dad, Kate & Fat around 7:30 P.M.

June 2. Sunday. Beautiful Day. All children home kept Gene, & Bob's to give me a "Welcome Celebration"

June 20. Got my 1st heart attack since over a year ago (last spring).

July 1940

July 10. 2nd heart attack since home & worse this time too.

July 30. 3rd heart attack since home & had to call the Priest.

August 1940

August 10. Vern's Birthday. Another heart attack. Found out I was to be disinherited. Ed & I.

August 20. Another Party told me he heard the same thing as mentioned in last entry. One Attack after another with each attack becoming more & more severe & serious. Don't believe I slept an hr or 2 at most on the average until both Mom & Dad told me that I was to receive at least the equivalent of $5000.00 as my share. Attacks becoming less severe & less frequent, been regaining my normal sleep one more & not so jittery anymore either.

DECEMBER 1940

December 25. Wed., cloudy, nice fair weather that eve. But becoming more windy. Receive a leather diary, carton cig. from Mom & Dad 4 Xmas. Cig from Vern & Ethel. Nice Day. MERRY XMAS TO ALL! All the girls & I chipped in & got Mom & Dad a 9 x 12 rug. Received a carton of cigs from Kate & Fat, Lidy & Gene, 2 paks from Mary, got 50 from Art & Vern. Also 2 pks. From Ann & Cyril. All home cept Ed & Dot, Fat, Gene, Cara & Bob's, & Gordon. Emptied 2 pints of whiskey. Went to confession & Communion and Mass of Dawn. Herb here too. Swell feed. Played cards.

Dec 26. Thurs. Cloudy. Ma making a quilt. Vern Ann, Hal helping. Got the chills twice last nite. Pretty bad too. Clara came & helped quilt too. Brot me 3 pks of cig 4 XMAS. Ann didn't come. Chills again too.

Dec 27. Fair. Friday. Got no chills 4 a change once. Pulse almost normal felt pretty good.

Dec 28. Sat. snowed & stormed Called Kirland yesterday for a script & it was sent to Fat by Gene. Picked up

Dec 29. Sun. Nice weather, thawed. Frank, Ethel, & Dad to church with Frank's jalopy. Brought Vern home too. Intence pain. & attack at 3:30 PM. Answered Fred Latimer's Post Card. Abs getting worse on L. knew & quite a bit of pain in both hands from steaming. Frank & Ethel & Son. Got Vern over to Lewis Leffler's this Eve. Got a terrible Attack.

Dec 30. Snowed & blowed a little. No Slip off & no chills. Vern playing again. Pain in L. knee.

Dec 31. Tuesday. Snowed & blowed. Snowplow opened our road. Got a good start of an Attack but got rid of it in time. Wrote a letter, Ray, Merlie & sent off Latiner's letter today too. Got 2 very bad attacks at night. Had 3 shots I lost during the Day. If only my attacks & wasted bangs would quit, I'd thank the Almighty. Had to cut out a needle I broke taking a shot. Made a crosscut before got it out.

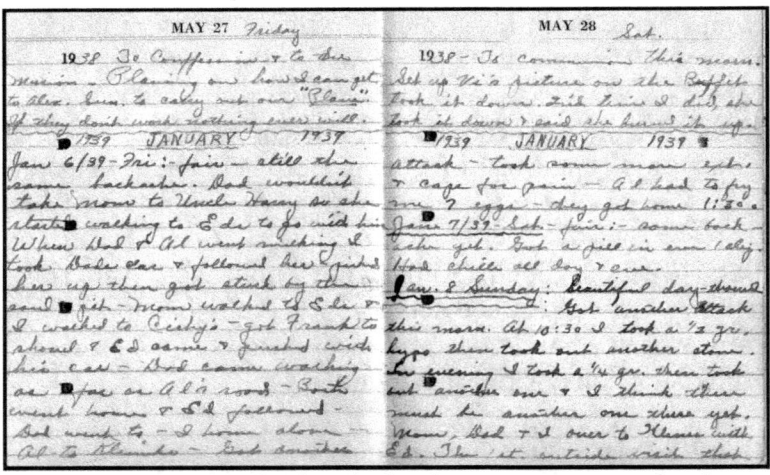

When Ray was finished with the diary, it was completely and entirely full, with no space to write anything more.

This concludes the entries from Violet's diary, used first by her, and after she died on October 17, 1938 in the auto accident, by Ray until December of 1940. His entry on December 25, 1940, says, "Received a diary...from mom and dad." But that diary has been lost, or perhaps he never wrote in it. Despite attempts to break Raymond of his drug habit at a site in Lexington, Kentucky—and thoughts of sending him to Germany, which didn't pan out--Ray's disease of Staphylococcus pyremia was too much, and he succumbed on June 6, 1941.

After Vi died, Ray continued to live in his parents' farm house, shown above on the right, until his 1941 death.

This listing of the deaths of people in the Seven Dolors Cemetery at Millerville, Minnesota, includes Raymond, the first on the list, who died of staphyloccus pyemia, and Violet, the third, who died of an auto accident.

Ray and Vi's gravestone in Seven Dolors Cemetery in Millerville, with their years of death—she 18 in 1938, and he, 24 years old in 1941.

Muriel Koeplin Keil, Ray's niece shown at 5 in 1941, knew him until he died that year.

www.ingramcontent.com/pod-product-compliance
Lightning Source LLC
LaVergne TN
LVHW020440070526
838199LV00063B/4792